Empathy
Readings for Writers

Edited by Magdalen Powers

Empathy: Readings for Writers

ISBN: 978-1-943536-43-6
Edition 1.0 Fall 2018

Chemeketa Press

Chemeketa Press is a nonprofit publishing endeavor at Chemeketa Community College that works with faculty, staff, and students to create affordable and effective alternatives to commercial textbooks. All proceeds from the sales of this textbook go toward the development of new textbooks. To learn more, visit www.chemeketapress.org

Publisher: Tim Rogers
Director: Steve Richardson
Managing Editor: Brian Mosher
Instructional Editor: Stephanie Lenox
Design Editor: Ronald Cox IV
Cover Design: Faith Martinmaas
Cover Photo: Golden Gate Bridge, by Casey Horner is in the public domain (https://unsplash.com/photos/-s8vX-XpGK4).
Interior Design: Mack Allen, Kristi Etzel, Emily Evans, Cassandra Johns,
    Jess Kolman, Erica Meyers

Chemeketa Faculty

The development of this text has benefited from the contributions of many Chemeketa faculty in addition to the editor, including:
    Alexis Butzner, Sara Dennison, Matthew Hodgson, Shannon Kelley, Brian
    Mosher, and Allison Tobey

Printed in the United States of America.

Contents

Introduction

What Is Empathy, and Why Do We Need This Book?

Homo sum: humani nil a me alienum puto.
I am human: nothing human is alien to me.
— *Terence (Publius Terentius Afer), c. 195/185–c. 159 BCE*

Terence was brought to Rome as a slave and became a playwright after he was freed by his master. Although Terence's words above express empathy, the word itself would not appear in English until two thousand years later (from the Greek word *empathia*, meaning "in feeling"). Whatever its origins, we now understand "empathy" to mean the act or capacity of experiencing someone else's feelings.

Empathy is considered a "soft skill," but that term masks the power of this important quality. How can we live up to our historic ideals of "liberty and justice for all" if we cannot understand the lived experiences of people who are not like us? While we have come a long way in the United States—for example, a hundred years ago, women couldn't vote, and Native Americans didn't have citizenship—we still have a long way to go toward living up to the ideals expressed in our country's founding documents.

As discrimination and hatred are currently front-page news, it felt necessary to compile an anthology that gave voice to these different experiences and perspectives. This book is far from perfect, even so, it offers a glimpse of others' lives that may be unlike our own but that are all part of the human experience. It asks readers to join "in

1

feeling" with these texts and to expand their idea of what it means to be human.

The current political climate isn't that unusual in the long view of human history. Tyrants come and go, conflicts flare and fade. But the hard work of coexistence never ends. It is vital that we take up this work, and it is vital that we do it today.

Magdalen Powers
Chemeketa Community College

Alien and Sedition Acts

These laws originated in the United States Senate and House of Representatives. In 1798, Congress passed acts to expand the ability of the government to deport or imprison non-citizens and criminalize certain types of speech against the government. Although neither of these acts are in force today, the sentiments expressed are still relevant to modern political discourse.

An Act Concerning Aliens

Section 1

Be it enacted by the Senate and the House of Representatives of the United States of America in Congress assembled, That it shall be lawful for the President of the United States at any time during the continuance of this act, to order all such aliens as he shall judge dangerous to the peace and safety of the United States, or shall have reasonable grounds to suspect are concerned in any treasonable or secret machinations against the government thereof, to depart out of the territory of the United States, within such time as shall be expressed in such order, which order shall be served on such alien by delivering him a copy thereof, or leaving the same at his usual abode, and returned to the office of the Secretary of State, by the marshal or other person to whom the same shall be directed. And in case any alien, so ordered to depart, shall be found at large within the United States after the time limited in such order for his departure, and not having obtained a license from the President to reside therein, or having obtained such license shall not have conformed thereto, every such alien shall, on conviction thereof, be imprisoned for a term not exceeding three years, and shall never after be admitted to become a citizen of the United States. Provided always, and be it further enacted, that if any alien so ordered to depart shall prove to the satisfaction of the President, by evidence to be taken before such person or persons as the President shall direct, who are for that purpose hereby authorized to administer oaths, that no injury or danger to the United States will arise from suffering such alien to reside therein, the President may grant a license to such alien to remain within the United States for such time as he shall judge proper, and at such place as he may designate. And the President may also require of such alien to enter into a bond to the United States, in such penal sum as he may direct, with one or more sufficient sureties to the satisfaction of the person authorized by the President to take the same, conditioned for the good behavior of such alien during his residence in the United States, and not violating his license, which license the President may revoke, whenever he shall think proper.

Section 2

And be it further enacted, That it shall be lawful for the President of the United States, whenever he may deem it necessary (for the public safety) to order to be removed out of the territory thereof, any alien who may or shall be in prison in pursuance of this act; and to cause to be arrested and sent out of the United States such of those aliens as shall have been ordered to depart therefrom and shall not have obtained a license as aforesaid, in all cases where, in the opinion of the President, the public safety requires a speedy removal. And if any alien so removed or sent out of the United States by the President shall voluntarily return thereto, unless by permission of the President of the United States, such alien on conviction thereof, shall be imprisoned so long as, in the opinion of the President, the public safety may require.

Section 3

And be it further enacted, That every master or commander of any ship or vessel which shall come into any port of the United States after the first day of July next, shall immediately on his arrival make report in writing to the collector or other chief officer of the customs of such port, of all aliens, if any, on board his vessel, specifying their names, age, the place of nativity, the country from which they shall have come, the nation to which they belong and owe allegiance, their occupation and a description of their persons, as far as he shall be informed thereof, and on failure, every such master and commander shall forfeit and pay three hundred dollars, for the payment whereof on default of such master or commander, such vessel shall also be holden, and may by such collector or other officer of the customs be detained. And it shall be the duty of such collector or other officer of the customs, forthwith to transmit to the office of the department of state true copies of all such returns.

Section 4

And be it further enacted, That the circuit and district courts of the United States, shall respectively have cognizance of all crimes and offences against this act. And all marshals and other officers of the United States are required to execute all precepts and orders of the President of the United States issued in pursuance or by virtue of this act.

Section 5

And be it further enacted, That it shall be lawful for any alien who may be ordered to be removed from the United States, by virtue of this act, to take with him such part of his goods, chattels, or other property, as he may find convenient; and all property left in the United States by any alien, who may be removed, as aforesaid, shall be, and remain subject to his order and disposal, in the same manner as if this act had not been passed.

Section 6

And be it further enacted, That this act shall continue and be in force for and during the term of two years from the passing thereof.

APPROVED, June 25, 1798.
John Adams
President of the United States.

An Act for the Punishment of Certain Crimes Against the United States

Section 1

Be it enacted by the Senate and House of Representatives of the United States of America, in Congress assembled, That if any persons shall unlawfully combine or conspire together, with intent to oppose any measure or measures of the government of the United States, which are or shall be directed by proper authority, or to impede the operation of any law of the United States, or to intimidate or prevent any person holding a place or office in or under the government of the United States, from undertaking, performing or executing his trust or duty, and if any person or persons, with intent as aforesaid, shall counsel, advise or attempt to procure any insurrection, riot, unlawful assembly, or combination, whether such conspiracy, threatening, counsel, advice, or attempt shall have the proposed effect or not, he or they shall be deemed guilty of a high misdemeanor, and on conviction, before any court of the United States having jurisdiction thereof, shall be punished by a fine not exceeding five thousand dollars, and by imprisonment during a term not less than six months nor exceeding five years; and further, at the discretion of the court may be holden to find sureties for his good behaviour in such sum, and for such time, as the said court may direct.

Section 2

And be it further enacted, That if any person shall write, print, utter or publish, or shall cause or procure to be written, printed, uttered or published, or shall knowingly and willingly assist or aid in writing, printing, uttering or publishing any false, scandalous and malicious writing or writings against the government of the United States, or either house of the Congress of the United States, or the President of the United States, with intent to defame the said government, or either house of the said Congress, or the said President, or to bring them, or either of them, into contempt or disrepute; or to excite against them, or either or any of them, the hatred of the good people of the United States, or to stir up sedition within the United States, or to excite any unlawful combinations therein, for opposing or resisting any law of the United States, or any act of the President of the United States, done in pursuance of any such law, or of the powers in him vested by the constitution of the United States, or to resist, oppose, or defeat any such law or act, or to aid, encourage or abet any hostile designs of any foreign nation against United States, their people or government, then such person, being thereof convicted before any court of the United States having jurisdiction thereof, shall be punished by a fine not exceeding two thousand dollars, and by imprisonment not exceeding two years.

Section 3

And be it further enacted and declared, That if any person shall be prosecuted under this act, for the writing or publishing any libel aforesaid, it shall be lawful for the defendant, upon the trial of the cause, to give in evidence in his defence, the truth of the matter contained in publication charged as a libel. And the jury who shall try the cause, shall have a right to determine the law and the fact, under the direction of the court, as in other cases.

Section 4

15   And be it further enacted, That this act shall continue and be in force until the third day of March, one thousand eight hundred and one, and no longer: Provided, that the expiration of the act shall not prevent or defeat a prosecution and punishment of any offence against the law, during the time it shall be in force.

    APPROVED, July 14, 1798
    John Adams
    President of the United States.

A Letter to My Old Master

Jourdon Anderson

Jourdon Anderson (1825–1907; also sometimes spelled "Jordan" or "Jordon") was born in Tennessee. After living half of his life as a slave, he was freed by US Army troops and resettled in Ohio, where he held various jobs before becoming a church sexton, from 1894 until his death. His letter—a noted example of satirical writing—was first published in the Cincinnati Commercial *newspaper in 1865.*

Dayton, Ohio
August 7, 1865
To My Old Master, Colonel P.H. Anderson, Big Spring, Tennessee

Sir: I got your letter, and was glad to find that you had not forgotten Jourdon, and that you wanted me to come back and live with you again, promising to do better for me than anybody else can. I have often felt uneasy about you. I thought the Yankees would have hung you long before this, for harboring Rebs they found at your house. I suppose they never heard about your going to Colonel Martin's to kill the Union soldier that was left by his company in their stable. Although you shot at me twice before I left you, I did not want to hear of your being hurt, and am glad you are still living. It would do me good to go back to the dear old home again, and see Miss Mary and Miss Martha and Allen, Esther, Green, and Lee. Give my love to them all, and tell them I hope we will meet in the better world, if not in this. I would have gone back to see you all when I was working in the Nashville Hospital, but one of the neighbors told me that Henry intended to shoot me if he ever got a chance.

5   I want to know particularly what the good chance is you propose
to give me. I am doing tolerably well here. I get twenty-five dollars
a month, with victuals and clothing; have a comfortable home for
Mandy — the folks call her Mrs. Anderson — and the children — Milly, Jane, and Grundy — go to school and are learning well. The teacher
says Grundy has a head for a preacher. They go to Sunday school,
and Mandy and me attend church regularly. We are kindly treated.
Sometimes we overhear others saying, "Them colored people were
slaves" down in Tennessee. The children feel hurt when they hear such
remarks; but I tell them it was no disgrace in Tennessee to belong to
Colonel Anderson. Many darkeys would have been proud, as I used
to be, to call you master. Now if you will write and say what wages
you will give me, I will be better able to decide whether it would be to
my advantage to move back again.

        As to my freedom, which you say I can have, there is nothing to
be gained on that score, as I got my free papers in 1864 from the Pro-
vost-Marshal-General of the Department of Nashville. Mandy says
she would be afraid to go back without some proof that you were
disposed to treat us justly and kindly; and we have concluded to test
your sincerity by asking you to send us our wages for the time we
served you. This will make us forget and forgive old scores, and rely
on your justice and friendship in the future. I served you faithfully
for thirty-two years, and Mandy twenty years. At twenty-five dollars a
month for me, and two dollars a week for Mandy, our earnings would
amount to eleven thousand six hundred and eighty dollars. Add to
this the interest for the time our wages have been kept back, and de-
duct what you paid for our clothing, and three doctor's visits to me,
and pulling a tooth for Mandy, and the balance will show what we
are in justice entitled to. Please send the money by Adams's Express,
in care of V. Winters, Esq., Dayton, Ohio. If you fail to pay us for

faithful labors in the past, we can have little faith in your promises in the future. We trust the good Maker has opened your eyes to the wrongs which you and your fathers have done to me and my fathers, in making us toil for you for generations without recompense. Here I draw my wages every Saturday night; but in Tennessee there was never any pay-day for the negroes any more than for the horses and cows. Surely there will be a day of reckoning for those who defraud the laborer of his hire.

In answering this letter, please state if there would be any safety for my Milly and Jane, who are now grown up, and both good-looking girls. You know how it was with poor Matilda and Catherine. I would rather stay here and starve—and die, if it come to that—than have my girls brought to shame by the violence and wickedness of their young masters. You will also please state if there has been any schools opened for the colored children in your neighborhood. The great desire of my life now is to give my children an education, and have them form virtuous habits.

Say howdy to George Carter, and thank him for taking the pistol from you when you were shooting at me.

From your old servant,
Jourdon Anderson

On Empathy

Marcus Aurelius

Marcus Aurelius (121–180 AD) was emperor of Rome from 161–180 CE. This excerpt is from Book 11 of his Meditations, *a series of personal notebooks not originally intended for publication. In this passage, he references the Muses of Greek mythology, nine goddesses who oversaw the arts and sciences, as he gives advice on how to deal with difficult people.*

As for other people's foolishness or wickedness, make sure it doesn't trouble or grieve you. If it does, first consider, "What is my relation to other people?" and that we are all born for the good of each other. . . .

Second, consider what type of people they are, at the table, in their beds, and so on—particularly how they are forced by their opinions to do what they do, and how proud they are of those acts.

Third, if people act according to what's right, you have no reason to be displeased. If they do not act rightly, they must be doing so against their will and through ignorance. According to the philosopher Plato, no one willingly does wrong. Therefore, people are grieved whenever they hear themselves called unjust, unconscionable, greedy, or are accused of acting wrongly toward their neighbors in any way.

Fourth, you yourself often do things wrong, and so you are human like everyone else. Even if you don't commit certain faults, you still have the disposition to commit them, although you are restrained because of fear, vanity, or some other ambitious, foolish quality.

5   Fifth, consider that you don't really know whether people are actually doing wrong or not. Many things are done in reference to circumstances, and generally a person must know a great deal about

12

those circumstances to judge another's actions.

Sixth, when you are upset with someone's actions, consider that life is short and that it is over quickly.

Seventh, consider that it isn't people's actions that disturb you but your own opinions of those actions. Take away your opinions, and your anger is gone. You may ask, "How, then, shall I take away these opinions?" By reflecting that the action itself hasn't shamed you. If shame is the only thing that can hurt you, you are sure to do many wrong things—to become a robber and anything else that will allow you to attain your worldly ends.

Eighth, consider how much more pain we feel from the anger and grief caused by someone's wrongful act than from the act itself.

Ninth, consider that a good disposition is invincible, if it is true and natural and not false or hypocritical. What will the most violent person do to you if you continue to be kind to them, and if, as the opportunity presents itself, you gently teach them to do better? "Not so, my child," you will say. "Nature made us for something else. I will not be hurt, but you are hurting yourself, my child." Then show that even bees don't act so poorly, nor do any other creatures that are naturally sociable. And you must do this without any harshness or rancor, but affectionately—not as if you were giving a lecture for the benefit of other people, but as if you were giving the advice to that person alone, even if there are other people around to hear.

Remember these nine rules as if you had received them from the nine Muses. See that you remember well and begin one day while you are still alive to be truly human. But you must equally remember not to flatter people or be angry at them, for both are uncharitable and lead to harm. And remember these rules even when you are angry, since to be angry is not noble, but to be meek and gentle is to be more human. Whoever possesses these qualities possesses strength, nerves,

10

and courage, while the person who is subject to fits of anger and dis-
content does not. The nearer the mind is to serenity, the nearer it is
to strength. As grief proceeds from weakness, so does anger. For those
who yield to pain and anger, both are wounded and both submit.

If you would have a tenth rule, it is this: Do not expect there to
be no wicked people in the world, because it is impossible; to allow
people to behave badly toward others while expecting them to not do
anything wrong to you shows the arrogance of a tyrant.

Sporting Faith

Dewnya Bakri-Bazzi

Dewnya Bakri-Bazzi is a co-founder of AT Law Group in Michigan. She was the first woman to wear a headscarf and play basketball. "Sporting Faith" first appeared in the 2011 anthology I Speak for Myself: American Women on Being Muslim.

"You cannot play in the tournament because your uniform does not conform to the rest of your team's uniform."

I was raised to be a God-loving individual, a person who under no circumstances should replace the Almighty as my number one priority. I would have never imagined this quality would become my biggest obstacle to participating in normal, everyday events in this free country of America.

Along with my strong religious beliefs comes the personal decision to maintain a conservative lifestyle. On a daily basis, I wear a scarf on my head, long-sleeved shirts up to my wrists, and full pants to my ankles. This includes my basketball uniform. I was eight years old when I first put on a scarf, and even though many coaches, referees, teammates, and even fans had a problem with it, I would not change my decision for the world.

Playing sports while wearing hijab is not a distraction or limitation as some may assume. When I played in tournaments and at other schools, however, it was a difficult task to make them understand the concept of the hijab. Many spectators refused to accept it. I would be stared at and talked about, but through it all, I never once thought to myself, "Maybe I should not have put a scarf on; maybe others are right, and it was not worth it." Instead, I took their negative attitudes as motivation. At the end of the day, it did not matter what I was wearing if I proved myself on the court. A good performance would in turn gain their respect. So every time I put on my Nikes, I knew I had something to prove. I knew I could not have too many off nights because each one represented a little respect lost—not only for me but for my religion. I was not only representing myself; I was also representing my faith.

5   My passion for basketball carried through to my college days at the University of Michigan, where I was a shooting guard for two years. The lack of respect for my uniform that I had experienced from fellow citizens, students, and teammates during the previous twelve years continued and even worsened in college. The coaches became less accepting, the referees became tougher, and the crowd became more hostile.

     Although the uniform I had been wearing for several years had been approved by the district board of athletics and the NAIA (National Association of Intercollegiate Athletics), I was forbidden by referees to play several games during my college career because of it. This helped me realize two things: 1) while I am being held back because of my religious beliefs, I must not be the only person who is experiencing this; and 2) although our constitution separates church from state and the courts recognize this difference, there are people out there who do not.

     "Why do you wear that scarf?"

     "Doesn't it choke you?"

     "Are you able to perform with it on?"

10   To my critics, my silent (and sometimes verbalized) answer was always, "Yes, I can! I can perform, and I will perform." I tried to be humble. I tried to address the critics in a way that was neither arrogant

nor aggressive. Yet they continued with their outrageous questions.

"Can you hear?"

"Can you see?"

"Doesn't it affect your peripheral vision?"

Then came the holy month of Ramadan. Many critics thought I was going to die because I would not eat or drink while taking part in conditioning drills. My teammates, however, were amazed. They asked questions "and thought I was so strong for being able to handle the workload with no food or water." Some of them even tried to fast for a day to see how it was. It was rewarding to see them trying to understand the concepts and to realize they respected my perseverance.

When I first joined my college team, my teammates thought Islam was a religion that preached violence, killing, and terrorism. Now, one year after my departure from the team, many of my former teammates are curious about Islam. They saw how I carried myself, were impressed by my disposition, and realized that if I represented Islam the way I did, it had to be a great religion. Peace, unity, kindness, helpfulness, and gratitude—all were virtues I talked about and tried to embody in my actions on and off the court. Through sheer action, I was able to change their minds about Islam and make them understand what our Prophet taught us.

I found both comfort and solidarity in helping a Christian teammate who believed she could only wear skirts based on her interpretation of the Bible. When dealing with the situation, she came to me for courage and asked me to enlighten her on how to get her dress code approved. I told her the steps she would have to take, and she is now playing basketball in a skirt. Even though this is not the same story as mine, she used me as a role model and a stepping stone to carry out her beliefs. My story is not unique. Every person tries to make their faith fit in with their everyday life.

I want to continue to make a difference. I want to help people. I want people to think, "Dewnya stood for what she believed in, and she succeeded." I want to help pass a far-reaching statute for all levels of sport and other daily activities that allows people to continue in their pursuits without thinking to themselves, "Do I need to change myself in order to . . . ?"

Over the years, I have grown to become what I believe is a good student, athlete, activist, person, and, most importantly, a follower of the truth. This experience has brought me to where I am today. By becoming a lawyer, I hope to help the Muslim community in several ways. One of my objectives is to advise Muslim business owners about how to operate their companies in ethical ways. Since September 11, 2001, the United States government has implemented several laws to prevent money laundering, terrorist funding, and similar activities. These laws, whether we like it or not, focus on the Muslim community. By undertaking ethical tactics and law-abiding policies within organized structures, we as a community can help discredit the bad reputation the government and media have tried to attach to the Muslim community.

All of my life, I have faced controversy "due to my religious beliefs." Inspired by my love of sports and sense of personal obligation to help others, I have never wavered in my aspirations to follow through with my goals and morals. The constant struggle to do what I love while concentrating on my "beliefs" was not easy. Many people may look at my story and feel it was not that big of a struggle, that I was playing sports the same as many other students do every day. My struggle was in dealing with those who believed a girl covered from head to toe could not and should not be a part of the world of sports.

20 When I was in the eighth grade, my athletic director and coach, Mr. Picanon, told me something that fueled my ambition for the rest

of my life: "Dewnya, you made history! First hijabi Female Athlete of the Year, first hijabi to earn your varsity letter in all four sports. You are truly an inspiration."

Five and Dime

Lewis Buzbee

Lewis Buzbee teaches in the Master of Fine Arts in Creative Writing pro-
gram at the University of San Francisco, where he lives and writes. "Five
and Dime" comes from his 2006 short-story collection, After the Gold
Rush.

You have to know how much I hate this. By the time I get to after-school, a little late, Sam's on the verge of tears. He's a big kid, nine,
but why shouldn't he cry? And he's still my baby. It's raining, pouring,
December dark, and after-school's been closed and locked for forty-five minutes. Sam knows that sometimes I'm late—it's happened
before—but still. I called the school to let them know, and like every
other time, they plead there's nothing they can do, they've got families,
too, he'll have to wait outside. He'll be okay, they tell me.

Sam's huddled under the little porch by the school's multipurpose
room, afraid to move away from the cone of light there, afraid of the
shadowy playground and the slick river of traffic beyond the fence.
He's got his backpack on, it drags him down, he's ready to go. When
he sees me, he bolts through the rain, his backpack bumping, he whispers Mom and runs right into my arms. I can feel the heat from his
face, feel the sob rise up in his chest, then he sighs and the evening
runs out of him, he collapses into me, uncurls. I hate this.

I have a pretty good deal at work, considering, but every so often
there's some sales report that can't possibly wait, and I have to stay
and tweak it, knowing full well the report will sit on Harmon's desk
all the next day, probably over the weekend, too. I mean, give me a

break. Even when I get out on time, I don't get to Sam until six, and he's stuck in after-school, reading, drawing, waiting. I imagine him waiting there with the other kids, every once in a while looking out the window, wondering if he'll ever get out.

And tonight has to be a Thursday, our special night, though not much of one. We take the train back to our neighborhood and go straight to the Five and Dime, eat grilled cheese at the counter, chocolate milkshake for dessert. Sam always gets to pick out a little something for himself.

I ask Sam if he still wants to go, maybe it's too late or too cold, and there's that sob again, clouding behind his eyes. He nods and nods, whispers a thin yes, then sees something in my look, and there goes the sob, winding out of him. We head for the train.   5

It's possible we moved into our neighborhood because of the Five and Dime. We'd been looking at apartments for days when we found this one, the one we're still in, a basement unit in the back, small and dark but nice enough, nice enough for Sam, little trooper, to call it rustic, a word I could not have imagined he'd know. I wanted to take the place immediately, out of sheer fatigue and hunger and a general pissiness that we had to do this at all, when Sam spotted the Five and Dime and its old-timey lunch counter and offered to buy me dinner. With his own money, his allowance. Now and then I have to remind myself that he's very sharp at reading other people, too good perhaps, too attentive.

Walking into Irving Variety Five and Dime was like stepping into my own past, and the first thing that told me this was the smell of the place, popcorn and butter and salted nuts, a bit of tang from the grill, the slight mustiness of things that haven't been moved in a while. There'd been a store like this in San Jose when I was growing up, a

Ben Franklin, and I'd stop there on the way home from school to buy candy or pencils, and sometimes with friends, in junior high mostly, we'd have lunch at the counter on weekends, feeling very grown-up. I bought my first bra there, without my mother knowing, ashamed to be buying it in such a store, not a department store, but relieved to be anonymous. The salesgirl wasn't much older than me, and she had bad skin and braces and seemed very unhappy, so it was perfect. The only time I ever tried to steal anything from anyone was from Ben Franklin, nail polish, Cherries in the Snow, but after walking around with it in my purse for a long time and pretending to be ruthlessly interested in every piece of merchandise in the store, I relented and put the polish back in its little rack, the end of my life of crime.

The day Sam and I first found Irving Variety was just like today, rainy and cold, the heart of winter's clipped days, two years ago now, and we both fell into the comfort of the place, the crowded aisles, the racks of cheap and cheerful and overlooked goods—tube socks, votive candles, ledgers, cookie cutters, jigsaw puzzles. I let Sam buy me dinner that first time. He was so proud of himself.

When we left that night, the little shopping street was all lit up, and we chased the shop windows in the rain, the shoemaker, the comics shop, the photo store, coin store, notary, a few cafes. We agreed to take the apartment, and I called the manager that night and wheedled and promised, and we got it. Paul had left us the year before and was living with his new girlfriend by then and she was already pregnant, so Sam and I had no choice but to move smaller. Paul and his new family could afford to move to Belvedere, in a big house that overlooked the bay and the city. With what I was making and the child support from Paul, Sam and I would just barely get by. That first year we were separated, Paul was super dad, taking Sam all the time and making promises to me about how good everything would turn out.

Then Debbie showed up, and they were pregnant and moving into the big house, and Sam and I were suddenly out of our lovely flat, and Paul decided it was best for Sam to stay with me in the city for school. Sam knew all too well what it meant, he'd have the bedroom, I'd sleep on the couch, and so he allowed the quiet charm of this poky little neighborhood to get to him. He made it appeal to him. All the merchants know Sam now, and if we miss a single Thursday night at Irving Variety's counter, they worry. We feel at home here.

The train comes up out of the tunnel into our neighborhood. The   10
rain's stopped and the sky's practically clear. But colder, too, really cold. The shop windows are all steamed up. I feel the skin on my face pinch. If I know anything about the weather here, all this points to a week of very cold and dry weather when the rain stops, it happens every year around this time. The problem is, we're not ready for this weather, don't have heavy coats and boots and gloves for the cold. This isn't Canada, after all. I'd prefer that it rain, swamp us, it's warmer that way.

Irving Variety is toasty inside, the ceiling heater blowing overtime. Dan and Treung, the owners, are behind the front counter, watching their small black and white, Wheel of Fortune, I think. They wave and call Sam over, offer him a toffee, a candy I know he doesn't like but which he dutifully accepts and pops in his mouth. He mumbles a thank you, and we all laugh a little. Like every Thursday.

Mrs. Park, cook and waitress, sees us, smiles broadly, then turns and begins to make our sandwiches. She knows what we'll have, there's no need to order. We sit on our usual stools at the far end of the counter, where we can watch everything come and go, keep an eye on who's passing by. Usually Sam and I spend dinner talking about the other customers, invent surprising histories for them. That one may look like an old lady, Sam'll say, but in reality she's a spy in the service of the evil Dr. Xanadu, and Sam, secret agent that he is, will have to save me from her evil clutches.

Tonight Sam goes on and on about the California mission system, and I'm happy to let him, and he's happy to tell me. They're studying how Spanish priests and soldiers made their way north from Baja and established a chain of small settlements. In the beginning it must have been so hard for them, Sam tells me, but they knew that one day they would build great cities here. Just think, Mom, he says, how far away they must have felt, Spain was far away, and all they had here was adobe and grass.

Over our shakes, Sam is telling Mrs. Park about the missions. He'll talk anyone's ear off. Mrs. Park nods and smiles and says, You don't say, which is how she keeps him talking. Sam draws a map for her, in crayon on one of the paper place mats. This is California, right?, he says, and see, they put the missions here and here and here, each one of them a day's horse ride from the other. They didn't have very much back then, especially the riders out on their own. They could only carry what they could carry, just enough to get them to the next outpost. You don't say, Mrs. Park says.

15 Later, Sam's glued to the glass cabinet of roasted nuts, and who can blame him. You can see the rich oils sweating out of the nuts, smell the dark surprise brought out by the hot lights in the case. They're expensive, I know that and Sam knows that, but it's been such a shitty day, why not. I order a half pound of cashews. Mrs. Park gently scoops the nuts out of their bin and empties them into a white paper bag. She hands me a chit and I go up front to pay. Sam hangs back in the toy section.

At the register I hand over the chit, fish out my wallet, and pay, and that's it, there's not a single bill left in there. Two quarters, we're done. Paul's check was supposed to be here Monday, but it wasn't, and when I called he apologized and told me it was on its way and it probably is. But still. I do get paid tomorrow but that's tomorrow and not tonight, and I'm the one who wants to break into tears now, there's not enough for the smallest trinket. I could charge it, but you know how that works, and I just don't know how much more into debt we can go.

Sam's standing by the wire rack of toys at the back of the aisle. These are the toys Sam's used to getting from me. Plastic paratroopers, jacks, Chinese jump rope, small bags of Army men, a stack of play money, glitzy crowns. Sam hands me the bag of cashews—he's saved my portion for me—then wipes his salty fingers on his pants before he picks up what he's been staring at. We've looked at this before, and I know he's wanted to get it but has been waiting for the right moment. Magic Crystal Garden, five-forty-nine, in a box about so big by so big. The picture on the box shows a Japanese looking rock garden with two bonsai trees growing out of it and between these a miniature Mt. Fuji that's supposed to be in the distance. You soak a cardboard skeleton of the garden in the solution, and over the next hour, the trees bloom and Mt. Fuji turns all blue and snow-capped. I suppose there's some educational value here, something about the science of minerals, but mostly it's cool looking.

Listen. I know Sam will be fine without this gewgaw, that his life would go on unimpeded, unharmed. And besides, at his father's on alternate weekends, he has more toys than a hundred kids could want. This is not a big deal. But I want him to have it, I want to get it for him tonight.

He's reading the directions on the back of the box now, and this means he wants it, he's made his choice. Do you want it, Sam, I ask, and the sound of his name in the air, unnecessary and unexpected, slays me. Oh yes, he says, always so polite. I take the box from him, tell him to keep looking while I pay.

20   They are so good to us here, I hate to do it, but in the housewares aisle, surrounded by cheap dishes and flimsy towels, I slip Sam's present deep into the bottom of my purse. I'll pay for it somehow.

After he's done with his homework, Sam readies the Magic Crystal Garden. He covers the kitchen table with newspapers taped together, and fills a Tupperware container with water. He mixes the galvanizing solution into the water, and we wait the required five minutes. Wearing my yellow dish gloves, he then immerses the skeleton of the garden, and we wait another ten minutes, which Sam fills by poring over the instruction booklet to find out as much as he can about the formation of these rudimentary patterns. Sam loves this line he finds in the instructions, Please to avoid rude accelerations, and we laugh and laugh, and cannot figure it out for the life of us.

Finally it's ready, and Sam gently removes the garden from the solution and sets it on its base. It may take, according to the fine print, as nearly as tall as two durable hours for full floweration. Sam's got an idea. He puts on a CD, The Beatles "Let It Be," his new favorite, then he grabs two storm candles from the kitchen, lights them and sets them on the kitchen table, and turns off all the lights. It's lovely. I turn up the heater a notch.

The Magic Crystal Garden begins to grow. On the black branches of the artificial trees, feathery shafts of matter begin to appear. Sam explains that it's magnetism of a sort, the crystal molecules aligning with one another, and in that alignment, parallel now, they accrue—he actually uses that word—and make new shapes where there's been nothing before. Mom, he says, it's simple, they push each other up.

The leaves of the tree are pink, the branches yellow, and the tiny flowers in the garden — not pictured on the box — are red and green. Mt. Fuji is the best, though. In the dim light of the storm candles it does seems far away, seems like a real mountain that's hazy and impossible to get to. You can almost see the unbroken trail of pilgrims winding their way, the ones who every day make their way to the top, for what? Is it heaven, they expect, nirvana? I love the view from here, the view of that distant mountain.

Cherokee Memorial

This memorial letter, written in December of 1829 to the United States Congress, was printed in January, 1830 in the Cherokee Phoenix, *the first American Indian newspaper. It was then reprinted in the March 13, 1830 issue of* Niles Weekly Register, *a periodical published in Baltimore, Maryland.*

To the honorable Senate and House of Representatives of the United States of America, in congress assembled:

The undersigned memorialists, humbly make known to your honorable bodies, that they are free citizens of the Cherokee nation. Circumstances of late occurrence have troubled our hearts, and induced us at this time to appeal to you, knowing that you are generous and just. . . .

By the will of our Father in heaven, the governor of the whole world, the red man of America has become small, and the white man great and renowned. When the ancestors of the people of these United States first came to the shores of America, they found the red man strong—though he was ignorant and savage, yet he received them kindly, and gave them dry land to rest their weary feet. They met in peace, and shook hands in token of friendship. Whatever the white man wanted and asked of the Indian, the latter willingly gave. At that time the Indian was the lord, and the white man the suppliant. But now the scene has changed. The strength of the red man has become weakness. As his neighbors increased in numbers, his power became less, and now, of the many and powerful tribes who once covered these United States, only a few are to be seen—a few whom a sweeping pestilence has left. The northern tribes, who were once so numerous and powerful, are now nearly extinct. Thus it has happened to the red man of America. Shall we, who are remnants, share the same fate?

Brothers—we address you according to usage adopted by our forefathers, and the great and good men who have successfully direct-ed the councils of the nation you represent—we now make known to you our grievances. We are troubled by some of your own people. Our neighbor, the state of Georgia, is pressing hard upon us, and urging us to relinquish our possessions for her benefit. We are told, if we do not leave the country, which we dearly love, and betake ourselves to the western wilds, the laws of the state will be extended over us, and the time, 1st of June, 1830, is appointed for the execution of the edict. When we first heard of this we were grieved and appealed to our father, the President, and begged that protection might be extended over us. But we were doubly grieved when we understood, from a letter of the Secretary of War to our Delegation, dated March of the present year [1829], that our father the President had refused us protection, and that he had decided in favor of the extension of the laws of the State over us. — This decision induces us to appeal to the immediate representatives of the American people. We love, we dearly love our country, and it is due to your honorable bodies, as well as to us, to make known why we think the country is ours, and why we wish to remain in peace where we are.

The land on which we stand, we have received as an inheritance   5 from our fathers, who possessed it from time immemorial, as a gift from our common father in heaven. We have already said, that when the white man came to the shores of America, our ancestors were found in peaceable possession of this very land. They bequeathed it to us as their children, and we have sacredly kept it as containing the remains of our beloved men. This right of inheritance we have never ceded, nor ever forfeited. Permit us to ask, what better right can a

people have to a country, than the right of inheritance and immemorial peaceable possession? We know it is said of late by the state of
Georgia, and by the executive of the United States, that we have forfeited this right—but we think this is said gratuitously. At what time
have we made the forfeit? What crime have we committed, whereby
we must forever be divested of our country and rights? Was it when
we were hostile to the United States, and took part with the king of
Great Britain, during the struggle for independence? If so, why was
not this forfeiture declared in the first treaty of peace between the
United States and our beloved men? . . .

In addition to that first of all rights, the right of inheritance and
peaceable possession, we have the faith and pledge of the U. States, repeated over and over again, in treaties made at various times. By these
treaties our rights as a separate people are distinctly acknowledged,
and guarantees given that they shall be secured and protected. So we
have always understood the treaties. The conduct of the government
towards us, from this organization until very lately, the talks given
to our beloved men by the presidents of the United States, and the
speeches of the agents and Commissioners, all concur to show that
we are not mistaken in our interpretation.—Some of our beloved
men who signed the treaties are still leaving [*sic*, living], and their testimony tends to the same conclusion. We have always supposed that
this understanding of the treaties was in accordance with the views
of the government; nor have we ever imagined that anybody would
interpret them otherwise. In what light shall we view the conduct of
the United States and Georgia, in their intercourse with us, in urging
us to enter into treaties, and cede lands? If we were but tenants at will,
why was it necessary that our consent must be obtained before these
governments could take lawful possession of our lands? The answer
is obvious. These governments perfectly understood our rights—our

right to the country, and our right to self government. Our understanding of the treaties is further supported by the intercourse law of the United States, which prohibits all encroachments upon our territory. The undersigned memorialists humbly represent, that if their interpretation of the treaties has been different from that of the government, then they have ever been deceived as to how the government regarded them, and what she asked and promised. Moreover, they have uniformly misunderstood their own acts.

In view of the strong ground upon which their rights are founded, your memorialists solemnly protest against being considered as tenants at will, or as mere occupants of the soil, without possessing the sovereignty. We have already stated to your honorable bodies, that our forefathers were found in possession of this soil in full sovereignty, by the first European settlers; and as we have never ceded nor forfeited the occupancy of the soil and the sovereignty over it, we do solemnly protest against being forced to leave it, either [by] direct or by indirect measures. To the land of which we are now in possession we are attached—it is our father's gift—it contains their ashes—it is the land of our nativity, and the land of our intellectual birth. We cannot consent to abandon it, for another far inferior, and which holds out to us no inducements. We do moreover protest against the arbitrary measures of our neighbor, the state of Georgia, in her attempt to extend her laws over us, in surveying our lands without our consent and in direct opposition to treaties and the intercourse law of the United States, and interfering with our municipal regulations in such a manner as to derange the regular operations of our own laws. To deliver and protect them from all these and every encroachment upon their rights, the undersigned memorialists do most earnestly pray your honorable bodies. Their existence and future happiness are at stake—divest them of their liberty and country, and you sink them in degradation, and put a check, if not a final stop, to their present progress in the arts of civilized life, and in the knowledge of the Christian religion. Your memorialists humbly conceive, that such an act would be in the highest degree oppressive. From the people of these United States, who perhaps, of all men under heaven, are the most religious and free, it cannot be expected. — Your memorialists, therefore, cannot anticipate such a result. You represent a virtuous, intelligent and Christian nation. To you they willingly submit their cause for your righteous decision.

Chinese Exclusion Act

This act of May 6, 1882, was the first significant immigration-restriction law in the United States. The Act prohibited the immigration of Chinese laborers for the next 10 years. Even Chinese who were already in the US, having played a large part in building the first transcontinental railroad, faced restrictions on re-entry. Chinese immigration was limited by law until the 1920s, and various other exclusion laws were in place until 1943.

An Act to Execute Certain Treaty Stipulations Relating to Chinese

Whereas, in the opinion of the Government of the United States the coming of Chinese laborers to this country endangers the good order of certain localities within the territory thereof: Therefore,

Be it enacted, That from and after the expiration of ninety days next after the passage of this act, and until the expiration of ten years next after the passage of this act, the coming of Chinese laborers to the United States be, . . . suspended; and during such suspension it shall not be lawful for any Chinese laborer to come, or, having so come after the expiration of said ninety days, to remain within the United States.

Section 2
That the master of any vessel who shall knowingly bring within the United States on such vessel, and land or permit to be landed, any Chinese laborer, from any foreign port or place, shall be deemed guilty of a misdemeanor, and on conviction thereof shall be punished by a fine of not more than five hundred dollars for each and every

such Chinese laborer so brought, and may be also imprisoned for a term not exceeding one year.

Section 3
That the two foregoing sections shall not apply to Chinese laborers who were in the United States on the seventeenth day of November, eighteen hundred and eighty, or who shall have come into the same before the expiration of ninety days next after the passage of this act. . . .

Section 6
5   That in order to the faithful execution of articles one and two of the treaty in this act before mentioned, every Chinese person other than a laborer who may be entitled by said treaty and this act to come within the United States, and who shall be about to come to the United States, shall be identified as so entitled by the Chinese Government in each case, such identity to be evidenced by a certificate issued under the authority of said government, which certificate shall be in the English language or (if not in the English language) accompanied by a translation into English, stating such right to come, and which certificate shall state the name, title, or official rank, if any, the age, height, and all physical peculiarities, former and present occupation or profession and place of residence in China of the person to whom the certificate is issued and that such person is entitled conformably to the treaty in this act mentioned to come within the Untied States. . . .

Section 12
That no Chinese person shall be permitted to enter the United States by land without producing to the proper office of customs the certificate in this act required of Chinese persons seeking to land from a vessel. Any Chinese person found unlawfully within the United States shall be caused to be removed therefrom to the country from whence

he came, by direction of the President of the United States, and at the cost of the United States, after being brought before some justice, judge, or commissioner of a court of the United States and found to be one not lawfully entitled to be or remain in the United States.

Section 13

That this act shall not apply to diplomatic and other officers of the Chinese Government traveling upon the business of that government, whose credentials shall be taken as equivalent to the certificate in this act mentioned, and shall exempt them and their body and household servants from the provisions of this act as to other Chinese persons.

Section 14

That hereafter no State court or court of the United States shall admit Chinese to citizenship; and all laws in conflict with this act are hereby repealed.

Section 15

That the words "Chinese laborers," whenever used in this act, shall be construed to mean both skilled and unskilled laborers and Chinese employed in mining.

Empathy for the Devil

By Wendy Chin-Tanner

Wendy Chin-Tanner is a poet who lives in upstate New York. She is the daughter of Chinese immigrants. This piece first appeared on AlterNet *in 2017.*

The first two weeks of Trump's presidency have proven to be everything liberal Americans have feared, and more. In addition to the heartrending scenes of deportation and detention at airports around the country last weekend, a revelation emerged from a Virginia courtroom Friday that more than 100,000 visas have been revoked as a result of Trump's notorious executive order. And the Migration Policy Institute reports that a leaked draft of a possible executive order on public benefits for cash, nutrition and health is set to have devastating effects on legal immigrants who rely on those vital services.

As the daughter of immigrants, my response to the travel ban and the heartening protests against it is strong, emotionally charged and personal. Like many of us, I've been taking to social media to air my views.

I posted this on Facebook:

"Bravissimo to the folks who are leveraging their citizenship privilege and white privilege to stand up against the immigration ban. But we have to get our facts straight about the history of immigration in America.

5   "America as a 'Melting Pot' welcoming all immigrants with open arms, where the 'American Dream' is equally accessible to all, is a myth. It's a myth that erases the colonization and genocide of Indigenous Americans, the forced migration and enslavement of African Americans, and bans against non-white immigrants that have happened before.

"Think of the Chinese Exclusion Act. Think of Japanese-American Internment. Think of the Jewish refugees we turned away during the Holocaust. Think of California's Proposition 187. Think of what Muslim Americans were subjected to after 9/11. Think of the inhumane way the ICE treats undocumented immigrants even in our so-called sanctuary cities.

"We don't need myths to unite us.

"The truth we have to reckon with is that America is a settler nation that has only truly welcomed white immigrants from European countries. Let's recognize that truth so that we can move on and make it not true anymore."

Then, after the Trump administration's warmongering against Iran and explicit talk of war with China, I posted this:

"War with China, any kind of war, whether trade war, skirmishes   10
in the South China Sea, or more, means unequivocally that Chinese Americans (and anybody else who looks remotely Chinese or has a Chinese-sounding last name) will be vilified, harassed, discriminated against, attacked, and killed.

"A cursory look at our history in America shows this to be true. The phrase 'a Chinaman's chance' wasn't coined for nothing. Our history is riddled with mass murders, anti-Chinese riots, lynchings, and hate crimes.

"Our only hope, as ever, is in intersectional allyship."

Sure enough, hate crimes against Asian Americans are surging, from the 60-year-old Chinese grandfather who was shot and killed in Virginia while playing Pokemon Go, to the Korean grandmother who was beaten in Los Angeles by a woman shouting "White power!"

While it has certainly been cathartic to publicly air my views, I'm also aware that I'm essentially preaching to the choir in my "liberal bubble." Ever since the election, we've been hearing calls for unity, empathy and healing. From Van Jones to President Obama, there's been a lot of talk about the need for empathy on all sides and about how to get out of our bubbles, whether liberal or conservative. And now, after the first two weeks of Trump's presidency, as we find ourselves staring into an honest to goodness existential abyss, the need to collectively grab the wheel and steer our country away from disaster is urgent.

15   From our respective bubbles, it's all too easy for us to demonize each other, dismissing opportunities to see and capitalize on the ways in which our views may even align. Righteous anger is legitimate, galvanizing and healthy, but how does anger square with empathy? Can we have empathy for people on the "other side" while still honoring our own emotions? Can we have empathy for the devil?

I've been doing a lot of thinking about these questions, especially since the Writers Resist Dear Sugar Radio broadcast where I helped give advice to a listener about how to have empathy and move on after the election.

Empathy-based radical practice has a long tradition in social justice activism from Gandhi to Martin Luther King, Jr., but as in those two examples, it has been embedded in religious and spiritual philosophies. As America is, at least for now, a secular society, is it possible to build a movement that has the empathy without the religion? In other words, can we come up with an organizational practice for the strategic application of empathy in a broad-based secular movement?

Like many of us, the place where I have occasion to practice empathy most often is in my marriage. If my husband and I have a disagreement, I don't have to sublimate my anger in order to listen to his point of view. For me to listen to him with empathy, I have to stand firm in my own position and express myself honestly, too. And part of the bargain is that he has to do the same thing. By staying clear and firm in the validity of my own experience, I can see how my husband's experience is distinct from mine, and from there, I can imagine how things might look and feel from where he stands. Rather than creating an impasse or stalemate, this process tends to actually build intimacy and respect.

The goal of a good marriage isn't never to argue. So maybe, just like in a marriage, we Americans should stop trying not to argue and instead try to argue well. That means fighting hard, but fighting fair. That means expressing ourselves honestly and then actively listening to the other person. Active listening is listening not with the goal of crafting a response or rebuttal, but listening with the simple goal of understanding where the other person is coming from.

Of course, that's not going to be possible 100 percent of the time. While arguing is healthy in a good marriage, arguing and even relationship therapy are contraindicated in abusive relationships because they can enable further abuse. The same can be said for any kind of abusive or oppressive situation. So how can we tell what kind of situation is safe and healthy to engage in and what kind of situation is dangerous and unproductive? How can we maintain our own position while understanding someone else's even if we are radically opposed? In other words, how does radical empathy work on a functional level?

What I propose is a two-step plan for radical empathy where step one is self empathy and step two is strategic empathy. What if self empathy means having empathy for ourselves, so that step one is to honor our own emotions even in the face of defensiveness, blame-shifting, minimization and gaslighting? Techniques like gaslighting, blame-shifting and minimizing create distance between our sense of self and our experience of reality. That's where empathy for the self comes in. When our sense of self is splintered by techniques designed to fracture us into a double positionality, even to the extent of manipulating us into identifying with abusers or oppressors, self empathy enables us to resist that pressure and empathize with the parts of ourselves that have been othered, whether by shame or alienation, or some other mode of manipulation. Self empathy prevents us from inadvertently colluding with oppressive narratives and internalizing their discourses. If we work from that basis, we can use self empathy as a tool for discerning what is and isn't productive to engage with, which in turn creates space for the possibility of step two, strategic empathy.

Strategic empathy is an idea that stems from the anthropological principle of cultural relativism. Not to be confused with moral relativism, cultural relativism is a tool for understanding the internal logic of different thought and belief systems even if they seem irrational to the researcher. The goal is then to develop culturally appropriate forms of intervention. If we adapt this approach to our current situation, we can use strategic empathy to help us maintain our own points of view while understanding the context and reasoning of someone else's even if we don't agree with them, even if we're angry at them, and even if we can't find it within ourselves to love them. From there, we have a starting point for finding the kinds of arguments and interventions that might actually get through to the people we're talking to.

When we're interacting with someone who's on the other side of the empathy wall, if we have no basis for understanding one another, it doesn't matter how many times we say something or how loudly we say it. They won't be able to hear us. Maybe this two-step radical empathy plan can at least get us to a point of having actual conversations (with those who are willing and capable) rather than debates and shouting matches.

We can see an example of how culturally appropriate interventions work in the research on political persuasion by Matt Feinberg, an assistant professor at the University of Toronto, who along with Stanford University sociologist Robb Willer, has studied how liberals and conservatives can convert people from the other side. As Olga Khazan reports in *The Atlantic,* the main obstacle is that people tend to present arguments that appeal only to the ethical code of their own side. However, through the use of "moral reframing" to more effectively craft convincing arguments based on frameworks that are culturally appropriate, Feinberg and Willer have shown that it's possible for liberals and conservatives to change each other's minds.

"We tend to view our moral values as universal," says Feinberg. "Yet, in order to use moral reframing you need to recognize that the other side has different values, know what those values are, understand them well enough to be able to understand the moral perspective of the other side, and be willing to use those values as part of a political argument." "To do so," continues Khazan, "would take an abundance of empathy, and that's in short supply all around these days."

It's certainly the case that many people, especially those on the far left, feel that the time for empathy is over. Ta-Nehisi Coates writes, for example, about how empathy is a privilege. Well, maybe it is and maybe now is the time to cash in on that privilege, not just to recognize it, but to leverage it.

Racism has become a word that makes people recoil and get defensive and say, "No, no, no, not me! How dare you!" But let's take it out of the personal context and look at it as a neutral systemic phenomenon. In critical race theory, the definition of racism is prejudice + power. What this means is that anyone can be prejudiced, but racism as a system only works if it has systemic power backing it up. And our country has that in spades. Similarly, sexism is prejudice + power. This means that women can be prejudiced against men (and other women), but without the whole setup backing them up, their prejudice is not technically sexism.

Racism and sexism are part of our cultural matrix along with classism, ableism, homophobia, transphobia, and other forms of discrimination. We're all in the matrix together. So those who can see the matrix would really benefit from working toward liberating those who can't see it yet. This idea forms the basis of intersectional social activism.

But even before we get into it with the Trump supporters, let's face the fact that we have plenty of divisions on our own side of the street. Everyone is triggered and everyone is defensive. So how do we get out of that state of stasis? How do we get someone to see something they don't want to see? Is it impossible? I don't think so, because don't most of us manage it with our kids and partners on a regular basis?

30   We know from child psychology that the development of empathy hinges on intimate and healing experiences of recognition. We grow empathy in children by mirroring to them that we understand and share their pain. Without empathy, we go into fight or flight states of hyper vigilance or are overwhelmed by feelings of hopelessness. Empathy depends on being accurately understood, but it doesn't depend on agreement. That's the key. We can have empathy for someone while still disagreeing with them. And once someone feels heard, they're in a much better position to hear us back. One of the best ways I've found to get my kids to understand a position that's opposed to their own is to tell them a story that helps them identify with a different point of view.

Now, most social justice activists would say that these aren't children we're dealing with and marginalized folks have already been called upon to do way too much heavy lifting in terms of empathy and emotional labor. And that's absolutely true.

But at the same time, people need imaginative bridges so that they can identify with positionalities and experiences that are outside of their own. Radical empathy is strategically beneficial because it allows us, without compromising ourselves, to meet people where they are and give them a place to go. If someone is painted into a corner, they're not going to come out. The absence of an active praxis in empathy results too often in mutual gaslighting because it's human nature to get defensive, double down, dismiss, and lash out when we feel threatened.

It's important to note that we must be mindful of how much capital we've got in our relative empathy accounts. People with more privilege should have more empathy to spend. If I'm in a position where I'm not immediately threatened and I have privilege relative to the person I'm trying to talk to, then maybe I'm in a better position to take the first step in listening. And if I'm in a position where I'm not immediately threatened and I have privilege relative to someone who is being threatened, it's my responsibility as an ally to step up and intervene.

Empathy hinges on emotional labor. To have empathy, we have to be able to practice active listening, be reflexive, self-critical, and be able to act on constructive criticism. In our culture, women are more readily expected to practice these skills and are socialized to do more emotional labor, which is why intersectional feminism is at the forefront of social justice allyship.

Men, on the other hand, aren't asked in our culture to do much emotional labor by anyone except, in some cases, their domestic partners. This makes me think that family and relationship counseling might be an effective model for understanding how to create a two-step plan for radical empathy that's intersectional. Because family counseling hinges on empathy as its basic tenet while acknowledging the differences of power that may exist between partners, the goal is

35

for both partners to be acknowledged, mirrored, and heard.

In my own marriage, for example, there are some stark inequities of power. I'm a woman and I'm a person of color. My husband is a man and he's white. Our marriage, especially now, would be in big trouble if we didn't explicitly acknowledge those power differences and reconfirm based on our respective levels of privilege what boundaries are appropriate for us and what roles we expect of each other when situations of discrimination or bigotry arise. We've had some pretty unsettling but ultimately intimacy building conversations in the past months as the election has brought external politics crashing through our door. Just because we treat each other as equals in our own home doesn't mean we are treated as equals outside of it. Now more than ever before, what the second-wave feminists said is true. The personal is political, and it's often painful to acknowledge that truth.

But empathy has to begin from a basis of truth. To begin the process of healing, we have to first reckon with the truth. Reckoning means naming and acknowledging the inherited inequities of power that we live with and acknowledging the internalization of those inequities. We have a complicated truth in our country. We have an intersectional truth.

It's true that we have racism and that creates certain experiences. It's true that we have sexism and that creates different experiences. It's true that we have economic inequalities that have created a struggling working class, some (though certainly not all) of whom are white and they are affected by yet another set of truths. The same goes for ableism, homophobia, transphobia, and on and on, in layer upon layer of truth.

We must be capable as a country of listening to the multiple truths of our intersectional society without privileging or compromising any of them. Maybe radical empathy will help us get there. Maybe then we won't need to have empathy for the devil because we will see that the devil doesn't exist.

The Story of an Hour

Kate Chopin

Kate Chopin (1850–1904) was a Louisiana writer of short stories and novels whose work prefigures that of modern feminist authors. "The Story of an Hour" was first published in Vogue *magazine in 1894. Its depiction of heterosexual marriage has remained controversial.*

Knowing that Mrs. Mallard was afflicted with a heart trouble, great care was taken to break to her as gently as possible the news of her husband's death.

It was her sister Josephine who told her, in broken sentences; veiled hints that revealed in half concealing. Her husband's friend Richards was there, too, near her. It was he who had been in the newspaper office when intelligence of the railroad disaster was received, with Brently Mallard's name leading the list of "killed." He had only taken the time to assure himself of its truth by a second telegram, and had hastened to forestall any less careful, less tender friend in bearing the sad message.

She did not hear the story as many women have heard the same, with a paralyzed inability to accept its significance. She wept at once, with sudden, wild abandonment, in her sister's arms. When the storm of grief had spent itself she went away to her room alone. She would have no one follow her.

There stood, facing the open window, a comfortable, roomy armchair. Into this she sank, pressed down by a physical exhaustion that haunted her body and seemed to reach into her soul.

5   She could see in the open square before her house the tops of trees

that were all aquiver with the new spring life. The delicious breath of rain was in the air. In the street below a peddler was crying his wares. The notes of a distant song which some one was singing reached her faintly, and countless sparrows were twittering in the eaves.

There were patches of blue sky showing here and there through the clouds that had met and piled one above the other in the west facing her window.

She sat with her head thrown back upon the cushion of the chair, quite motionless, except when a sob came up into her throat and shook her, as a child who has cried itself to sleep continues to sob in its dreams.

She was young, with a fair, calm face, whose lines bespoke repression and even a certain strength. But now there was a dull stare in her eyes, whose gaze was fixed away off yonder on one of those patches of blue sky. It was not a glance of reflection, but rather indicated a suspension of intelligent thought.

There was something coming to her and she was waiting for it, fearfully. What was it? She did not know; it was too subtle and elusive to name. But she felt it, creeping out of the sky, reaching toward her through the sounds, the scents, the color that filled the air.

Now her bosom rose and fell tumultuously. She was beginning to   10
recognize this thing that was approaching to possess her, and she was striving to beat it back with her will—as powerless as her two white slender hands would have been. When she abandoned herself a little whispered word escaped her slightly parted lips. She said it over and over under her breath: "free, free, free!" The vacant stare and the look of terror that had followed it went from her eyes. They stayed keen and bright. Her pulses beat fast, and the coursing blood warmed and relaxed every inch of her body.

She did not stop to ask if it were or were not a monstrous joy that held her. A clear and exalted perception enabled her to dismiss the suggestion as trivial. She knew that she would weep again when she saw the kind, tender hands folded in death; the face that had never looked save with love upon her, fixed and gray and dead. But she saw beyond that bitter moment a long procession of years to come that would belong to her absolutely. And she opened and spread her arms out to them in welcome.

There would be no one to live for during those coming years; she would live for herself. There would be no powerful will bending hers in that blind persistence with which men and women believe they have a right to impose a private will upon a fellow-creature. A kind intention or a cruel intention made the act seem no less a crime as she looked upon it in that brief moment of illumination.

And yet she had loved him—sometimes. Often she had not. What did it matter! What could love, the unsolved mystery, count for in the face of this possession of self-assertion which she suddenly recognized as the strongest impulse of her being!

"Free! Body and soul free!" she kept whispering.

15   Josephine was kneeling before the closed door with her lips to the keyhole, imploring for admission. "Louise, open the door! I beg; open the door—you will make yourself ill. What are you doing, Louise? For heaven's sake open the door."

"Go away. I am not making myself ill." No; she was drinking in a very elixir of life through that open window.

Her fancy was running riot along those days ahead of her. Spring days, and summer days, and all sorts of days that would be her own. She breathed a quick prayer that life might be long. It was only yesterday she had thought with a shudder that life might be long.

She arose at length and opened the door to her sister's importunities. There was a feverish triumph in her eyes, and she carried herself unwittingly like a goddess of Victory. She clasped her sister's waist, and together they descended the stairs. Richards stood waiting for them at the bottom.

Some one was opening the front door with a latchkey. It was Brently Mallard who entered, a little travel-stained, composedly carrying his grip-sack and umbrella. He had been far from the scene of the accident, and did not even know there had been one. He stood amazed at Josephine's piercing cry; at Richards' quick motion to screen him from the view of his wife.

But Richards was too late. When the doctors came they said she had died of heart disease — of joy that kills.   20

Journal of the First Voyage to America, 1492–1493

Christopher Columbus

Cristoforo Columbo (c. 1451–1506) was an Italian explorer who is widely credited with having "discovered America." His voyages began the process of permanent European colonization of the New World. From 1492 to 1499, he served as the first governor of the Indies, appointed by Queen Isabella I of Spain.

In the name of our Lord Jesus Christ

Whereas, Most Christian, High, Excellent, and Powerful Princes, King and Queen of Spain and of the Islands of the Sea, our Sovereigns, this present year 1492, after your Highnesses had terminated the war with the Moors reigning in Europe, the same having been brought to an end in the great city of Granada, where on the second day of January, this present year, I saw the royal banners of your Highnesses planted by force of arms upon the towers of the Alhambra, which is the fortress of that city, and saw the Moorish king come out at the gate of the city and kiss the hands of your Highnesses, and of the Prince my Sovereign; and in the present month, in consequence of the information which I had given your Highnesses respecting the countries of India and of a Prince, called Great Can, which in our language signifies King of Kings, how, at many times he, and his predecessors had sent to Rome soliciting instructors who might teach him our holy faith, and the holy Father had never granted his request, whereby great numbers of people were lost, believing in idolatry and doctrines of perdition. Your Highnesses, as Catholic Christians, and

princes who love and promote the holy Christian faith, and are enemies of the doctrine of Mahomet, and of all idolatry and heresy, determined to send me, Christopher Columbus, to the above-mentioned
countries of India, to see the said princes, people, and territories, and
to learn their disposition and the proper method of converting them
to our holy faith; and furthermore directed that I should not proceed
by land to the East, as is customary, but by a Westerly route, in which
direction we have hitherto no certain evidence that any one has gone.
So after having expelled the Jews from your dominions, your Highnesses, in the same month of January, ordered me to proceed with a
sufficient armament to the said regions of India, and for that purpose
granted me great favors, and ennobled me that thenceforth I might
call myself Don, and be High Admiral of the Sea, and perpetual Vice-
roy and Governor in all the islands and continents which I might discover and acquire, or which may hereafter he discovered and acquired
in the ocean; and that this dignity should be inherited by my eldest
son, and thus descend from degree to degree forever. Hereupon I left
the city of Granada, on Saturday, the twelfth day of May, 1492, and
proceeded to Palos, a seaport, where I armed three vessels, very fit
for such an enterprise, and having provided myself with abundance
of stores and seamen, I set sail from the port, on Friday, the third of
August, half an hour before sunrise, and steered for the Canary Islands
of your Highnesses which are in the said ocean, thence to take my
departure and proceed till I arrived at the Indies, and perform the
embassy of your Highnesses to the Princes there, and discharge the
orders given me. For this purpose I determined to keep an account of
the voyage, and to write down punctually every thing we performed
or saw from day to day, as will hereafter appear. Moreover, Sovereign
Princes, besides describing every night the occurrences of the day, and
every day those of the preceding night, I intend to draw up a nautical

chart, which shall contain the several parts of the ocean and land in their proper situations; and also to compose a book to represent the whole by picture with latitudes and longitudes, on all which accounts it behooves me to abstain from my sleep, and make many trials in navigation, which things will demand much labor.

Friday, 3 August 1492. Set sail from the bar of Saltes at 8 o'clock, and proceeded with a strong breeze till sunset, sixty miles or fifteen leagues south, afterwards southwest and south by west, which is the direction of the Canaries.

Monday, 6 August. The rudder of the caravel Pinta became loose, being broken or unshipped. It was believed that this happened by the contrivance of Gomez Rascon and Christopher Quintero, who were on board the caravel, because they disliked the voyage. The Admiral says he had found them in an unfavorable disposition before setting out. He was in much anxiety at not being able to afford any assistance in this case, but says that it somewhat quieted his apprehensions to know that Martin Alonzo Pinzon, Captain of the Pinta, was a man of courage and capacity. Made a progress, day and night, of twenty-nine leagues.

Thursday, 9 August. The Admiral did not succeed in reaching the island of Gomera till Sunday night. Martin Alonzo remained at Grand Canary by command of the Admiral, he being unable to keep the other vessels company. The Admiral afterwards returned to Grand Canary, and there with much labor repaired the Pinta, being assisted by Martin Alonzo and the others; finally they sailed to Gomera. They saw a great eruption of names from the Peak of Teneriffe, a lofty mountain. The Pinta, which before had carried latine sails, they altered and made her square-rigged. Returned to Gomera, Sunday, 2 September, with the Pinta repaired.

The Admiral says that he was assured by many respectable Span- 5
iards, inhabitants of the island of Ferro, who were at Gomera with
Dona Inez Peraza, mother of Guillen Peraza, afterwards first Count of
Gomera, that every year they saw land to the west of the Canaries; and
others of Gomera affirmed the same with the like assurances. The Admiral here says that he remembers, while he was in Portugal, in 1484,
there came a person to the King from the island of Madeira, soliciting
for a vessel to go in quest of land, which he affirmed he saw every year,
and always of the same appearance. He also says that he remembers
the same was said by the inhabitants of the Azores and described as in
a similar direction, and of the same shape and size. Having taken in
food, water, meat and other provisions, which had been provided by
the men which he left ashore on departing for Grand Canary to repair
the Pinta, the Admiral took his final departure from Gomera with the
three vessels on Thursday, 6 September.

Sunday, 9 September. Sailed this day nineteen leagues, and determined
to count less than the true number, that the crew might not be dismayed if the voyage should prove long. In the night sailed one hundred and twenty miles, at the rate of ten miles an hour, which make
thirty leagues. The sailors steered badly, causing the vessels to fall to
leeward toward the northeast, for which the Admiral reprimanded
them repeatedly.

Monday, 10 September. This day and night sailed sixty leagues, at the
rate of ten miles an hour, which are two leagues and a half. Reckoned
only forty-eight leagues, that the men might not be terrified if they
should be long upon the voyage.

Tuesday, 11 September. Steered their course west and sailed above twenty leagues; saw a large fragment of the mast of a vessel, apparently of a hundred and twenty tons, but could not pick it up. In the night sailed about twenty leagues, and reckoned only sixteen, for the cause above stated.

Friday, 14 September. Steered this day and night west twenty leagues; reckoned somewhat less. The crew of the Nina stated that they had seen a grajao, and a tropic bird, or water-wagtail, which birds never go farther than twenty-five leagues from the land.

10   *Sunday, 16 September.* Sailed day and night, west thirty-nine leagues, and reckoned only thirty-six. Some clouds arose and it drizzled. The Admiral here says that from this time they experienced very pleasant weather, and that the mornings were most delightful, wanting nothing but the melody of the nightingales. He compares the weather to that of Andalusia in April. Here they began to meet with large patches of weeds very green, and which appeared to have been recently washed away from the land; on which account they all judged themselves to be near some island, though not a continent, according to the opinion of the Admiral, who says, "the continent we shall find further ahead."

Monday, 17 September. Steered west and sailed, day and night, above fifty leagues; wrote down only forty-seven; the current favored them. They saw a great deal of weed which proved to be rockweed, it came from the west and they met with it very frequently. They were of opinion that land was near. The pilots took the sun's amplitude, and found that the needles varied to the northwest a whole point of the compass; the seamen were terrified, and dismayed without saying why. The Admiral discovered the cause, and ordered them to take the amplitude again the next morning, when they found that the needles were true; the cause was that the star moved from its place, while the needles remained stationary. At dawn they saw many more weeds, apparently river weeds, and among them a live crab, which the Admiral kept, and says that these are sure signs of land, being never found eighty leagues out at sea. They found the sea-water less salt since they left the Canaries, and the air more mild. They were all very cheerful, and strove which vessel should outsail the others, and be the first to discover land; they saw many tunnies, and the crew of the Nina killed one. The Admiral here says that these signs were from the west, "where I hope that high God in whose hand is all victory will speedily direct us to land." This morning he says he saw a white bird called a water- wagtail, or tropic bird, which does not sleep at sea.

19 September. Continued on, and sailed, day and night, twenty-five leagues, experiencing a calm. Wrote down twenty-two. This day at ten o'clock a pelican came on board, and in the evening another; these birds are not accustomed to go twenty leagues from land. It drizzled without wind, which is a sure sign of land. The Admiral was unwilling to remain here, beating about in search of land, but he held it for certain that there were islands to the north and south, which in fact was the case and he was sailing in the midst of them. His wish was to proceed on to the Indies, having such fair weather, for if it please God, as the Admiral says, we shall examine these parts upon our return. Here the pilots found their places upon the chart: the reckoning of the Nina made her four hundred and forty leagues distant from the Canaries, that of the Pinta four hundred and twenty, that of the Admiral four hundred.

Thursday, 20 September. Steered west by north, varying with alternate changes of the wind and calms; made seven or eight leagues' progress. Two pelicans came on board, and afterwards another,–a sign of the neighborhood of land. Saw large quantities of weeds today, though none was observed yesterday. Caught a bird similar to a grajao; it was a river and not a marine bird, with feet like those of a gull. Towards night two or three land birds came to the ship, singing; they disappeared before sunrise. Afterwards saw a pelican coming from west-northwest and flying to the southwest; an evidence of land to the westward, as these birds sleep on shore, and go to sea in the morning in search of food, never proceeding twenty leagues from the land.

Friday, 21 September. Most of the day calm, afterwards a little wind. Steered their course day and night, sailing less than thirteen leagues. In the morning found such abundance of weeds that the ocean seemed to be covered with them; they came from the west. Saw a pelican; the sea smooth as a river, and the finest air in the world. Saw a whale, an indication of land, as they always keep near the coast.

15 *Saturday, 22 September.* Steered about west-northwest varying their course, and making thirty leagues' progress. Saw few weeds. Some pardelas were seen, and another bird. The Admiral here says "this headwind was very necessary to me, for my crew had grown much alarmed, dreading that they never should meet in these seas with a fair wind to return to Spain." Part of the day saw no weeds, afterwards great plenty of it.

Sunday, 23 September. Sailed northwest and northwest by north and at times west nearly twenty-two leagues. Saw a turtle dove, a pelican, a river bird, and other white fowl;–weeds in abundance with crabs among them. The sea being smooth and tranquil, the sailors murmured, saying that they had got into smooth water, where it would never blow to carry them back to Spain; but afterwards the sea rose without wind, which astonished them. The Admiral says on this occasion "the rising of the sea was very favorable to me, as it happened formerly to Moses when he led the Jews from Egypt."

Tuesday, 25 September. Very calm this day; afterwards the wind rose. Continued their course west till night. The Admiral held a conversation with Martin Alonzo Pinzon, captain of the Pinta, respecting a chart which the Admiral had sent him three days before, in which it appears he had marked down certain islands in that sea; Martin Alonzo was of opinion that they were in their neighborhood, and the Admiral replied that he thought the same, but as they had not met with them, it must have been owing to the currents which had carried them to the northeast and that they had not made such progress as the pilots stated. The Admiral directed him to return the chart, when he traced their course upon it in presence of the pilot and sailors.

At sunset Martin Alonzo called out with great joy from his vessel that he saw land, and demanded of the Admiral a reward for his intelligence. The Admiral says, when he heard him declare this, he fell on his knees and returned thanks to God, and Martin Alonzo with his crew repeated Gloria in excelsis Deo, as did the crew of the Admiral. Those on board the Nina ascended the rigging, and all declared they saw land. The Admiral also thought it was land, and about twenty-five leagues distant. They remained all night repeating these affirmations, and the Admiral ordered their course to be shifted from west to southwest where the land appeared to lie. They sailed that day four leagues and a half west and in the night seventeen leagues southwest, in all twenty-one and a half: told the crew thirteen leagues, making it a point to keep them from knowing how far they had sailed; in this manner two reckonings were kept, the shorter one falsified, and the other being the true account. The sea was very smooth and many of the sailors went in it to bathe, saw many dories and other fish.

Wednesday, 26 September. Continued their course west till the afternoon, then southwest and discovered that what they had taken for land was nothing but clouds. Sailed, day and night, thirty- one leagues; reckoned to the crew twenty-four. The sea was like a river, the air soft and mild.

Sunday, 30 September. Continued their course west and sailed day and night in calms, fourteen leagues; reckoned eleven.–Four tropic birds came to the ship, which is a very clear sign of land, for so many birds of one sort together show that they are not straying about, having lost themselves. Twice, saw two pelicans; many weeds. The constellation called Las Gallardias, which at evening appeared in a westerly direction, was seen in the northeast the next morning, making no more progress in a night of nine hours, this was the case every night, as says the Admiral. At night the needles varied a point towards the northwest, in the morning they were true, by which it appears that the polar star moves, like the others, and the needles are always right.

20   *Monday, 1 October.* Continued their course west and sailed twenty-five leagues; reckoned to the crew twenty. Experienced a heavy shower. The pilot of the Admiral began to fear this morning that they were five hundred and seventy-eight leagues west of the island of Ferro. The short reckoning which the Admiral showed his crew gave five hundred and eighty-four, but the true one which he kept to himself was seven hundred and seven leagues.

Saturday, 6 October. Continued their course west and sailed forty leagues day and night; reckoned to the crew thirty-three. This night Martin Alonzo gave it as his opinion that they had better steer from west to southwest. The Admiral thought from this that Martin Alonzo did not wish to proceed onward to Cipango; but he considered it best to keep on his course, as he should probably reach the land sooner in that direction, preferring to visit the continent first, and then the islands.

Sunday, 7 October. Continued their course west and sailed twelve miles an hour, for two hours, then eight miles an hour. Sailed till an hour after sunrise, twenty-three leagues; reckoned to the crew eighteen. At sunrise the caravel Nina, who kept ahead on account of her swiftness in sailing, while all the vessels were striving to outsail one another, and gain the reward promised by the King and Queen by first discovering land–hoisted a flag at her mast head, and fired a lombarda, as a signal that she had discovered land, for the Admiral had given orders to that effect. He had also ordered that the ships should keep in close company at sunrise and sunset, as the air was more favorable at those times for seeing at a distance. Towards evening seeing nothing of the land which the Nina had made signals for, and observing large flocks of birds coming from the North and making for the southwest, whereby it was rendered probable that they were either going to land to pass the night, or abandoning the countries of the north, on account of the approaching winter, he determined to alter his course, knowing also that the Portuguese had discovered most of the islands they possessed by attending to the flight of birds. The Admiral accordingly shifted his course from west to west-southwest, with a resolution to continue two days ill that direction. This was done about an hour after sunset. Sailed in the night nearly five leagues, and twenty-three in the day. In all twenty-eight.

Monday, 8 October. Steered west-southwest and sailed day and night eleven or twelve leagues; at times during the night, fifteen miles an hour, if the account can be depended upon. Found the sea like the river at Seville, "thanks to God," says the Admiral. The air soft as that of Seville in April, and so fragrant that it was delicious to breathe it. The weeds appeared very fresh. Many land birds, one of which they took, flying towards the southwest; also grajaos, ducks, and a pelican were seen.

Tuesday, 9 October. Sailed southwest five leagues, when the wind changed, and they stood west by north four leagues. Sailed in the whole day and night, twenty leagues and a half; reckoned to the crew seventeen. All night heard birds passing.

25   *Wednesday, 10 October.* Steered west-southwest and sailed at times ten miles an hour, at others twelve, and at others, seven; day and night made fifty-nine leagues' progress; reckoned to the crew but forty-four. Here the men lost all patience, and complained of the length of the voyage, but the Admiral encouraged them in the best manner he could, representing the profits they were about to acquire, and adding that it was to no purpose to complain, having come so far, they had nothing to do but continue on to the Indies, till with the help of our Lord, they should arrive there.

Thursday, 11 October. Steered west-southwest; and encountered a heavier sea than they had met with before in the whole voyage. Saw pardelas and a green rush near the vessel. The crew of the Pinta saw a cane and a log; they also picked up a stick which appeared to have been carved with an iron tool, a piece of cane, a plant which grows on land, and a board. The crew of the Nina saw other signs of land, and a stalk loaded with rose berries. These signs encouraged them, and they all grew cheerful. Sailed this day till sunset, twenty-seven leagues.

After sunset steered their original course west and sailed twelve miles an hour till two hours after midnight, going ninety miles, which are twenty-two leagues and a half; and as the Pinta was the swiftest sailer, and kept ahead of the Admiral, she discovered land and made the signals which had been ordered. The land was first seen by a sailor called Rodrigo de Triana, although the Admiral at ten o'clock that evening standing on the quarter-deck saw a light, but so small a body that he could not affirm it to be land; calling to Pero Gutierrez, groom of the King's wardrobe, he told him he saw a light, and bid him look that way, which he did and saw it; he did the same to Rodrigo Sanchez of Segovia, whom the King and Queen had sent with the squadron as comptroller, but he was unable to see it from his situation. The Admiral again perceived it once or twice, appearing like the light of a wax candle moving up and down, which some thought an indication of land. But the Admiral held it for certain that land was near; for which reason, after they had said the Salve which the seamen are accustomed to repeat and chant after their fashion, the Admiral directed them to keep a strict watch upon the forecastle and look out diligently for land, and to him who should first discover it he promised a silken jacket, besides the reward which the King and Queen had offered, which was an annuity of ten thousand maravedis. At two o'clock in the morning the land was discovered, at two leagues' distance; they took in sail and remained under the square-sail lying to till day, which was Friday, when they found themselves near a small island, one of the Lucayos, called in the Indian language Guanahani. Presently they descried people, naked, and the Admiral landed in the boat, which was armed, along with Martin Alonzo Pinzon, and Vincent Yanez his brother, captain of the Nina. The Admiral bore the royal standard, and the two captains each a banner of the Green Cross, which all the ships had carried; this contained the initials of the names of the King and Queen each side of the cross, and a crown over each letter. Arrived on shore, they saw trees very green many streams of water, and diverse sorts of fruits. The Admiral called upon the two Captains, and the rest of the crew who landed, as also to Rodrigo de Escovedo notary of the fleet, and Rodrigo Sanchez, of Segovia, to bear witness that he before all others took possession (as in fact he did) of that island for the King and Queen his sovereigns, making the requisite declarations, which are more at large set down here in writing. Numbers of the people of the island straightway collected together. Here follow the precise words of the Admiral: "As I saw that they were very friendly to us, and perceived that they could be much more easily converted to our holy faith by gentle means than by force, I presented them with some red caps, and strings of beads to wear upon the neck, and many other trifles of small value, wherewith they were much delighted, and became wonderfully attached to us. Afterwards they came swimming to the boats, bringing parrots, balls of cotton thread, javelins, and many other things which they exchanged for articles we gave them, such as glass beads, and hawk's bells; which trade was carried on with the utmost good will. But they seemed on the whole to me, to be a very poor people. They all go completely naked, even the women, though I saw but one girl. All whom I saw were young, not above thirty years of age, well made, with fine shapes and faces; their hair short, and coarse like that of a horse's tail, combed toward the forehead, except a small portion which they suffer to hang down behind, and never cut. Some paint themselves with black, which makes them appear like those of the Canaries, neither black nor white; others with white, others with red, and others with such colors as they can find. Some paint the face, and some the whole body; others only the eyes, and others the nose.

Weapons they have none, nor are acquainted with them, for I showed them swords which they grasped by the blades, and cut themselves through ignorance. They have no iron, their javelins being without it, and nothing more than sticks, though some have fish-bones or other things at the ends. They are all of a good size and stature, and handsomely formed. I saw some with scars of wounds upon their bodies, and demanded by signs the of them; they answered me in the same way, that there came people from the other islands in the neighborhood who endeavored to make prisoners of them, and they defended themselves. I thought then, and still believe, that these were from the continent. It appears to me, that the people are ingenious, and would be good servants and I am of opinion that they would very readily become Christians, as they appear to have no religion. They very quickly learn such words as are spoken to them. If it please our Lord, I intend at my return to carry home six of them to your Highnesses, that they may learn our language. I saw no beasts in the island, nor any sort of animals except parrots." These are the words of the Admiral.

Saturday, 13 October. At daybreak great multitudes of men came to the shore, all young and of fine shapes, very handsome; their hair not curled but straight and coarse like horse-hair, and all with foreheads and heads much broader than any people I had hitherto seen; their eyes were large and very beautiful; they were not black, but the color of the inhabitants of the Canaries, which is a very natural circumstance, they being in the same latitude with the island of Ferro in the Canaries. They were straight-limbed without exception, and not with prominent bellies but handsomely shaped. They came to the ship in canoes, made of a single trunk of a tree, wrought in a wonderful manner considering the country; some of them large enough to contain forty or forty-five men, others of different sizes down to those fitted to hold but a single person. They rowed with an oar like a baker's peel, and wonderfully swift. If they happen to upset, they all jump into the sea, and swim till they have righted their canoe and emptied it with the calabashes they carry with them. They came loaded with balls of cotton, parrots, javelins, and other things too numerous to mention; these they exchanged for whatever we chose to give them. I was very attentive to them, and strove to learn if they had any gold. Seeing some of them with little bits of this metal hanging at their noses, I gathered from them by signs that by going southward or steering round the island in that direction, there would be found a king who possessed large vessels of gold, and in great quantities. I endeavored to procure them to lead the way thither, but found they were unacquainted with the route. I determined to stay here till the evening of the next day, and then sail for the southwest; for according to what I could learn from them, there was land at the south as well as at the southwest and northwest and those from the northwest came many times and fought with them and proceeded on to the southwest in search of gold and precious stones. This is a large and level island, with trees extremely flourishing, and streams of water; there is a large lake in the middle of the island, but no mountains: the whole is completely covered with verdure and delightful to behold. The natives are an inoffensive people, and so desirous to possess any thing they saw with us, that they kept swimming off to the ships with whatever they could find, and readily bartered for any article we saw fit to give them in return, even such as broken platters and fragments of glass. I saw in this manner sixteen balls of cotton thread which weighed above twenty-five pounds, given for three Portuguese ceutis. This traffic I forbade, and suffered no one to take their cotton from them, unless I should order it to be procured for your Highnesses, if proper quantities could be met with. It grows in this island, but from my short stay here I could not satisfy myself fully concerning it; the gold, also, which they wear in their noses, is found here, but not to lose time, I am determined to proceed onward and ascertain whether I can reach Cipango. At night they all went on shore with their canoes.

Sunday, 14 October. In the morning, I ordered the boats to be got ready, and coasted along the island toward the north-northeast to examine that part of it, we having landed first at the eastern part. Presently we discovered two or three villages, and the people all came down to the shore, calling out to us, and giving thanks to God. Some brought us water, and others victuals: others seeing that I was not disposed to land, plunged into the sea and swam out to us, and we perceived that they interrogated us if we had come from heaven. An old man came on board my boat; the others, both men and women cried with loud voices–"Come and see the men who have come from heavens. Bring them victuals and drink." There came many of both sexes, every one bringing something, giving thanks to God, prostrating themselves on the earth, and lifting up their hands to heaven. They called out to us loudly to come to land, but I was apprehensive on account of a reef of rocks, which surrounds the whole island, although within there is depth of water and room sufficient for all the ships of Christendom, with a very narrow entrance. There are some shoals withinside, but the water is as smooth as a pond. It was to view these parts that I set out in the morning, for I wished to give a complete relation to your Highnesses, as also to find where a fort might be built. I discovered a tongue of land which appeared like an island though it was not, but might be cut through and made so in two days; it contained six houses. I do not, however, see the necessity of fortifying the place, as the people here are simple in war-like matters, as your Highnesses will see by those seven which I have ordered to be taken and carried to Spain in order to learn our language and return, unless your Highnesses should choose to have them all transported to Castile, or held captive in the island. I could conquer the whole of them with fifty men, and govern them as I pleased. Near the islet I have mentioned were groves of trees, the most beautiful I have ever seen, with their foliage as verdant as we see in Castile in April and May. There were also many streams. After having taken a survey of these parts, I returned to the ship, and setting sail, discovered such a number of islands that I knew not which first to visit; the natives whom I had taken on board informed me by signs that there were so many of them that they could not be numbered; they repeated the names of more than a hundred. I determined to steer for the largest, which is about five leagues from San Salvador; the others were some at a greater, and some at a less distance from that island. They are all very level, without mountains, exceedingly fertile and populous, the inhabitants living at war with one another, although a simple race, and with delicate bodies.

15 October. Stood off and on during the night, determining not to come to anchor till morning, fearing to meet with shoals; continued our course in the morning; and as the island was found to be six or seven leagues distant, and the tide was against us, it was noon when we arrived there. I found that part of it towards San Salvador extending from north to south five leagues, and the other side which we coasted along, ran from east to west more than ten leagues. From this island espying a still larger one to the west, I set sail in that direction and kept on till night without reaching the western extremity of the island, where I gave it the name of Santa Maria de la Concepcion. About sunset we anchored near the cape which terminates the island towards the west to enquire for gold, for the natives we had taken from San Salvador told me that the people here wore golden bracelets upon their arms and legs. I believed pretty confidently that they had invented this story in order to find means to escape from us, still I determined to pass none of these islands without taking possession, because being once taken, it would answer for all times. We anchored and remained till Tuesday, when at daybreak I went ashore with the boats armed. The people we found naked like those of San Salvador, and of the same disposition. They suffered us to traverse the island, and gave us what we asked of them. As the wind blew southeast upon the shore where the vessels lay, I determined not to remain, and set out for the ship. A large canoe being near the caravel Nina, one of the San Salvador natives leaped overboard and swam to her; (another had made his escape the night before,) the canoe being reached by the fugitive, the natives rowed for the land too swiftly to be overtaken; having landed, some of my men went ashore in pursuit of them, when they abandoned the canoe and fled with precipitation; the canoe which they had left was brought on board the Nina, where from another quarter had arrived a small canoe with a single man, who came to barter some cotton; some of the sailors finding him unwilling to go on board the vessel, jumped into the sea and took him. I was upon the quarter deck of my ship, and seeing the whole, sent for him, and gave him a red cap, put some glass beads upon his arms, and two hawk's bells upon his ears. I then ordered his canoe to be returned to him, and despatched him back to land.

I now set sail for the other large island to the west and gave orders for the canoe which the Nina had in tow to be set adrift. I had refused to receive the cotton from the native whom I sent on shore, although he pressed it upon me. I looked out after him and saw upon his landing that the others all ran to meet him with much wonder. It appeared to them that we were honest people, and that the man who had escaped from us had done us some injury, for which we kept him

30

in custody. It was in order to favor this notion that I ordered the canoe to be set adrift, and gave the man the presents above mentioned, that when your Highnesses send another expedition to these parts it may meet with a friendly reception. All I gave the man was not worth four maravedis. We set sail about ten o'clock, with the wind southeast and stood southerly for the island I mentioned above, which is a very large one, and where according to the account of the natives on board, there is much gold, the inhabitants wearing it in bracelets upon their arms, legs, and necks, as well as in their ears and at their noses. This island is nine leagues distant from Santa Maria in a westerly direction. This part of it extends from northwest, to southeast and appears to be twenty-eight leagues long, very level, without any mountains, like San Salvador and Santa Maria, having a good shore and not rocky, except a few ledges under water, which renders it necessary to anchor at some distance, although the water is very clear, and the bottom may be seen. Two shots of a lombarda from the land, the water is so deep that it cannot be sounded; this is the case in all these islands. They are all extremely verdant and fertile, with the air agreeable, and probably contain many things of which I am ignorant, not inclining to stay here, but visit other islands in search of gold. And considering the indications of it among the natives who wear it upon their arms and legs, and having ascertained that it is the true metal by showing them some pieces of it which I have with me, I cannot fail, with the help of our Lord, to find the place which produces it.

Being at sea, about midway between Santa Maria and the large island, which I name Fernandina, we met a man in a canoe going from Santa Maria to Fernandina; he had with him a piece of the bread which the natives make, as big as one's fist, a calabash of water, a quantity of reddish earth, pulverized and afterwards kneaded up, and some dried leaves which are in high value among them, for a quantity of it was brought to me at San Salvador; he had besides a little basket made after their fashion, containing some glass beads, and two blancas by all which I knew he had come from San Salvador, and had passed from thence to Santa Maria. He came to the ship and I caused him to be taken on board, as he requested it; we took his canoe also on board and took care of his things. I ordered him to be presented with bread and honey, and drink, and shall carry him to Fernandina and give him his property, that he may carry a good report of us, so that if it please our Lord when your Highnesses shall send again to these regions, those who arrive here may receive honor, and procure what the natives may be found to possess.

Tuesday, 16 October. Set sail from Santa Maria about noon, for Fernandina which appeared very large in the west; sailed all the day with calms, and could not arrive soon enough to view the shore and select a good anchorage, for great care must be taken in this particular, lest the anchors be lost. Beat up and down all night, and in the morning arrived at a village and anchored. This was the place to which the man whom we had picked up at sea had gone, when we set him on shore. He had given such a favorable account of us, that all night there were great numbers of canoes coming off to us, who brought us water and other things. I ordered each man to be presented with something, as strings of ten or a dozen glass beads apiece, and thongs of leather, all which they estimated highly; those which came on board I directed should be fed with molasses. At three o'clock, I sent the boat on shore for water; the natives with great good will directed the men where to find it, assisted them in carrying the casks full of it to the boat, and seemed to take great pleasure in serving us. This is a very large island, and I have resolved to coast it about, for as I understand, in, or near the island, there is a mine of gold. It is eight leagues west of Santa

Maria, and the cape where we have arrived, and all this coast extends from north-northwest to south-southeast. I have seen twenty leagues of it, but not the end. Now, writing this, I set sail with a southerly wind to circumnavigate the island, and search till we can find Samoet, which is the island or city where the gold is, according to the account of those who come on board the ship, to which the relation of those of San Salvador and Santa Maria corresponds. These people are similar to those of the islands just mentioned, and have the same language and customs; with the exception that they appear somewhat more civilized, showing themselves more subtle in their dealings with us, bartering their cotton and other articles with more profit than the others had experienced. Here we saw cotton cloth, and perceived the people more decent, the women wearing a slight covering of cotton over the nudities. The island is verdant, level and fertile to a high degree; and I doubt not that grain is sowed and reaped the whole year round, as well as all other productions of the place. I saw many trees, very dissimilar to those of our country, and many of them had branches of different sorts upon the same trunk; and such a diversity was among them that it was the greatest wonder in the world to behold. Thus, for instance, one branch of a tree bore leaves like those of a cane, another branch of the same tree, leaves similar to those of the lentisk. In this manner a single tree bears five or six different kinds. Nor is this done by grafting, for that is a work of art, whereas these trees grow wild, and the natives take no care about them. They have no religion, and I believe that they would very readily become Christians, as they have a good understanding. Here the fish are so dissimilar to ours that it is wonderful. Some are shaped like dories, of the finest hues in the world, blue, yellow, red, and every other color, some variegated with a thousand different tints, so beautiful that no one on beholding them could fail to express the highest wonder and admiration. Here are also whales. Beasts, we saw none, nor any creatures on land save parrots and lizards, but a boy told me he saw a large snake. No sheep nor goats were seen, and although our stay here has been short, it being now noon, yet were there any, I could hardly have failed of seeing them. The circumnavigation of the island I shall describe afterward.

Wednesday, 17 October. At noon set sail from the village where we had anchored and watered. Kept on our course to sail round the island; the wind southwest and south. My intention was to follow the coast of the island to the southeast as it runs in that direction, being informed by the Indians I have on board, besides another whom I met with here, that in such a course I should meet with the island which they call Samoet, where gold is found. I was further informed by Martin Alonzo Pinzon, captain of the Pinta, on board of which I had sent three of the Indians, that he had been assured by one of them I might sail round the island much sooner by the northwest. Seeing that the wind would not enable me to proceed in the direction I first contemplated, and finding it favorable for the one thus recommended me, I steered to the northwest and arriving at the extremity of the island at two leagues' distance, I discovered a remarkable haven with two entrances, formed by an island at its mouth, both very narrow, the inside capacious enough for a hundred ships, were there sufficient depth of water. I thought it advisable to examine it, and therefore anchored outside, and went with the boats to sound it, but found the water shallow. As I had first imagined it to be the mouth of a river, I had directed the casks to be carried ashore for water, which being done we discovered eight or ten men who straightway came up to us, and directed us to a village in the neighborhood; I accordingly dispatched the crews thither in quest of water, part of them armed, and the rest with the casks, and the place being at some distance it detained me here a couple of hours. In the meantime I strayed about among the groves, which present the most enchanting sight ever witnessed, a degree of verdure prevailing like that of May in Andalusia, the trees as different from those of our country as day is from night, and the same may be said of the fruit, the weeds, the stones and everything else. A few of the trees, however, seemed to be of a species similar to some that are to be found in Castile, though still with a great dissimilarity, but the others so unlike, that it is impossible to find any resemblance in them to those of our land. The natives we found like those already described, as to personal appearance and manners, and naked like the rest. Whatever they possessed, they bartered for what we chose to give them. I saw a boy of the crew purchasing javelins of them with bits of platters and broken glass. Those who went for water informed me that they had entered their houses and found them very clean and neat, with beds and coverings of cotton nets. Their houses are all built in the shape of tents, with very high chimneys. None of the villages which I saw contained more than twelve or fifteen of them. Here it was remarked that the married women wore cotton breeches, but the younger females were without them, except a few who were as old as eighteen years. Dogs were seen of a large and small size, and one of the men had hanging at his nose a piece of gold half as big as a castel-lailo, with letters upon it. I endeavored to purchase it of them in order to ascertain what sort of money it was but they refused to part with it. Having taken our water on board, I set sail and proceeded northwest till I had surveyed the coast to the point where it begins to run from east to west. Here the Indians gave me to understand that this island was smaller than that of Samoet, and that I had better return in order to reach it the sooner. The wind died away, and then sprang up from the west-northwest which was contrary to the course we were pursuing, we therefore hove about and steered various courses through the night from east to south standing off from the land, the weather being cloudy and thick. It rained violently from midnight till near day, and the sky still remains clouded; we remain off the southeast part of the island, where I expect to anchor and stay till the weather grows clear, when I shall steer for the other islands I am in quest of. Every day that I have been in these Indies it has rained more or less. I assure your Highnesses that these lands are the most fertile, temperate, level and beautiful countries in the world.

Thursday, 18 October. As soon as the sky grew clear, we set sail and went as far round the island as we could, anchoring when we found it inconvenient to proceed. I did not, however, land. In the morning we set sail again.

Friday, 19 October. In the morning we got under weigh, and I ordered the Pinta to steer east and southeast and the Nina south-southeast; proceeding myself to the southeast the other vessels I directed to keep on the courses prescribed till noon, and then to rejoin me. Within three hours we descried an island to the east toward which we directed our course, and arrived all three, before noon, at the northern extremity, where a rocky islet and reef extend toward the North, with another between them and the main island. The Indians on board the ships called this island Saomete. I named it Isabela. It lies westerly from the island of Fernandina, and the coast extends from the islet twelve leagues, west, to a cape which I called Cabo Hermoso, it being a beautiful, round headland with a bold shore free from shoals. Part of the shore is rocky, but the rest of it, like most of the coast here, a sandy beach. Here we anchored till morning. This island is the most beautiful that I have yet seen, the trees in great number, flourishing and lofty; the land is higher than the other islands, and exhibits an eminence, which though it cannot be called a mountain, yet adds a beauty to its appearance, and gives an indication of streams of water in the interior. From this part toward the northeast is an extensive bay with many large and thick groves. I wished to anchor there, and land, that I might examine those delightful regions, but found the coast shoal, without a possibility of casting anchor except at a distance from the shore. The wind being favorable, I came to the Cape, which I named Hermoso, where I anchored today. This is so beautiful a place, as well as the neighboring regions, that I know not in which course to proceed first; my eyes are never tired with viewing such delightful verdure, and of a species so new and dissimilar to that of our country, and I have no doubt there are trees and herbs here which would be of great value in Spain, as dyeing materials, medicine, spicery, etc., but I am mortified that I have no acquaintance with them. Upon our arrival here we experienced the most sweet and delightful odor from the flowers or trees of the island. Tomorrow morning before we depart, I intend to land and see what can be found in the neighborhood. Here is no village, but farther within the island is one, where our Indians inform us we shall find the king, and that he has much gold. I shall penetrate so far as to reach the village and see or speak with the king, who, as they tell us, governs all these islands, and goes dressed, with a great deal of gold about him. I do not, however, give much credit to these accounts, as I understand the natives but imperfectly, and perceive them to be so poor that a trifling quantity of gold appears to them a great amount. This island appears to me to be a separate one from that of Saomete, and I even think there may be others between them. I am not solicitous to examine particularly everything here, which indeed could not be done in fifty years, because my desire is to make all possible discoveries, and return to your Highnesses, if it please our Lord, in April. But in truth, should I meet with gold or spices in great quantity, I shall remain till I collect as much as possible, and for this purpose I am proceeding solely in quest of them.

Saturday, 20 October. At sunrise we weighed anchor, and stood to the 35
northeast and east along the south side of this island, which I named Isabela, and the cape where we anchored, Cabo de la Laguna; in this direction I expected from the account of our Indians to find the capital and king of the island. I found the coast very shallow, and offering every obstacle to our navigation, and perceiving that our course this way must be very circuitous, I determined to return to the westward. The wind failed us, and we were unable to get near the shore before night; and as it is very dangerous anchoring here in the dark, when it is impossible to discern among so many shoals and reefs whether the ground be suitable, I stood off and on all night. The other vessels came to anchor, having reached the shore in season. As was customary among us, they made signals to me to stand in and anchor, but I determined to remain at sea.

Sunday, 21 October. At 10 o'clock, we arrived at a cape of the island, and anchored, the other vessels in company. After having dispatched a meal, I went ashore, and found no habitation save a single house, and that without an occupant; we had no doubt that the people had fled in terror at our approach, as the house was completely furnished. I suffered nothing to be touched, and went with my captains and some of the crew to view the country. This island even exceeds the others in beauty and fertility. Groves of lofty and flourishing trees are abundant, as also large lakes, surrounded and overhung by the foliage, in a most enchanting manner. Everything looked as green as in April in Andalusia. The melody of the birds was so exquisite that one was never willing to part from the spot, and the flocks of parrots obscured the heavens. The diversity in the appearance of the feathered tribe from those of our country is extremely curious. A thousand different sorts of trees, with their fruit were to be met with, and of a wonderfully delicious odor. It was a great affliction to me to be ignorant of their natures, for I am very certain they are all valuable; specimens of them and of the plants I have preserved. Going round one of these lakes, I saw a snake, which we killed, and I have kept the skin for your Highnesses; upon being discovered he took to the water, whither we followed him, as it was not deep, and dispatched him with our lances; he was seven spans in length; I think there are many more such about here. I discovered also the aloe tree, and am determined to take on board the ship tomorrow, ten quintals of it, as I am told it is valuable. While we were in search of some good water, we came upon a village of the natives about half a league from the place where the ships lay; the inhabitants on discovering us abandoned their houses, and took to flight, carrying of their goods to the mountain. I ordered that nothing which they had left should be taken, not even the value of a pin. Presently we saw several of the natives advancing towards our party, and one of them came up to us, to whom we gave some hawk's bells and glass beads, with which he was delighted. We asked him in return, for water, and after I had gone on board the ship, the natives came down to the shore with their calabashes full, and showed great pleasure in presenting us with it. I ordered more glass beads to be given them, and they promised to return the next day. It is my wish to fill all the water casks of the ships at this place, which being executed, I shall depart immediately, if the weather serve, and sail round the island, till I succeed in meeting with the king, in order to see if I can acquire any of the gold, which I hear he possesses. Afterwards I shall set sail for another very large island which I believe to be Cipango, according to the indications I receive from the Indians on board. They call the Island

Colba, and say there are many large ships, and sailors there. This other island they name Bosio, and inform me that it is very large; the others which lie in our course, I shall examine on the passage, and according as I find gold or spices in abundance, I shall determine what to do; at all events I am determined to proceed on to the continent, and visit the city of Guisay, where I shall deliver the letters of your Highnesses to the Great Can, and demand an answer, with which I shall return.

The Other Edition

Kate Carroll de Gutes

Kate Carroll de Gutes is a Portland writer whose book Objects in Mirror Are Closer Than They Appear *won the 2016 Oregon Book Award for Creative Nonfiction and a 2016 Lambda Literary Award in Memoir. Her critically acclaimed blog,* The Authenticity Experiment, *is being adapted into a book.*

You probably are too young to remember it. Or maybe you didn't live in Portland then. Or maybe I am just making assumptions about who you are, how old you are, how long you've been in Portland (where the young go to retire). But there was a bad time here. I mean, afraid to walk to your black Ford Ranger pickup in the dark bad time. I mean, triple check the door locks bad time. I mean, can we afford an alarm service bad time. I mean, spit on and called "dyke" right on Hawthorne Boulevard bad time.

Yeah, that's right—on Hawthorne Boulevard, some men in a red pickup sped by my wife, our golden retriever and me, and shouted "Dykes!" out the truck window and spat at us. I think I remember wiping my cheek and forehead, but that's probably not true. I mean, that guy would have had to have been a precision spitter to hit me from a moving vehicle. What I do remember is the fear in my body, the way my shoulders came up and cramped, the way my eyes blinked closed and opened and then closed again, the way a shiver ran down my whole body and my pecs contracted hard—heart armor—and how I pushed my dog and my wife away from the edge of the curb, reflexively, toward the relative safety of a cement wall three feet from the street.

It was 1992, worse, at least initially, than 2017, worse than we imagined the Cheeto Administration might be. Lon Mabon and his gang of thugs introduced Measure 9, a ballot initiative that equated homosexuality with pedophilia, necrophilia, and bestiality. The Measure stated, "Every public school shall recognize homosexuality as abnormal, wrong, unnatural, and perverse." You can't imagine it now, can you? Now that I am out in the world in a tie and boots, my hair cut short, shorter, shortest, faded up the back with a razor. But back then, in 1992, we were all mostly in the closet. That sounds so strange today—I can hardly remember what we were afraid of.

Okay, that's not true. I can remember what terrified us. The loss of family, of friends. The terrible fear of hate crimes. In 1992, 81% of LGBT people surveyed across America reported some sort of harassment; 36% were followed or chased; 31% reported physical violence. Two women shot on the Appalachian Trail by a man stalking them for hours. A woman in Central a Oregon campground run over by a truck and then almost hacked to death by a man swinging an axe at her tent over and over again. Two women in Medford bound, gagged, and shot in the head. Gay bashing as public sport, gay bashing more acceptable than overt racism.

Every day some new commercial or news story aired. Mabon, the   5
mastermind behind the campaign said, "What I'm trying to get you to see is that this is a war and we must fight it as such." A television news station interviewed a local school boy who was visiting an Anne Frank exhibit which had traveled to Portland. The boy said, "Jewish people are citizens. You know, it's totally different when you're beating up a gay person than when you're beating up a total citizen."

We owned a business, we owned a home, my wife worked at a Catholic hospital. Being out in 1992 meant potentially losing your job, or your business, possibly being forced from your neighborhood.

Four years earlier, when we'd begun the search for a house, the real estate agent asked us what would happen if one of us were to marry. We allowed as how this wouldn't be a problem. She asked why. I can remember hardly knowing what to say. "It just won't be," I stammered, my flaming cheeks answering the question more articulately than my words. Still, the bank insisted I write a letter proclaiming I would always rent a room from my "roommate," that I could not foresee moving from the house that would soon become "home" to my wife and me.

This is why we didn't come out. Even though Donna Redwing, one of our respected—and out—elders said, "Coming out is the most important political act in your life and you better do it now, or you may never have the opportunity again." This is why a group of us gathered on our front porch late one night, sitting on the swing made with hand tools by my wife's grandfather, leaning against the wide, white 2×8 rail top, and talking in low voices about when to come out, how to come out, who to come out to, strategizing. And when our fundamentalist neighbor walked by, one of my friends dove under the swing and crouched in the dark corner of the porch, out of line of sight. We joke about it now, laugh in that way that you laugh about old trauma, but you can't know the fear, the fear of gathering together like that and being identified.

Or maybe you do know what it is like. Maybe you are a person of color. Maybe you look "other" to the Cheeto in Chief and his henchmen. The Cheeto is no different than Lon Mabon was—both men fear-stricken bullies, both red heads with bad haircuts covering their bald spots. Today, the target has changed. Now I can wear a tie, while someone else cannot kneel on a small rug four times a day and pray towards Mecca or safely attend a pool party in their own neighborhood. Now, I can write about my wife, my ex-wife, and my girlfriends, and I can tell you that I am a genderqueer butch while someone else must stay quiet about their immigration status or their H1b visa.

"What I'm trying to get you to see is that this is a war and we must fight it as such." I will tell you, we are not winning the war right now—it's been less than a year since Orlando, and just last month a shooter opened fire in a mosque, and yesterday the House voted to take healthcare away from 25 million people. And, until we get our stories out there, until we come out again and again, come out about everything—sexuality, gender orientation, religion, race, politics, in-come—until we come out to everyone, there will always be a war because there will always be an other.

I'll start. My name is Kate and I'm a genderqueer butch who   10
lights a candle on her altar each day and prays to a higher power called Sophia. Al-anon and therapy, and bikes and my crazy quilt of friends have saved my life more times than I can count.

So who are you?

The Other Side of Loss

Rene Denfeld

Rene Denfeld is a licensed investigator and writer living in Portland with her three children, whom she adopted from foster care. Her first novel, the critically acclaimed The Enchanted, *was based on her many years working with death-row inmates. "The Other Side of Loss," which deals graphically with suicide, was first published in 2015.*

I come from a family of suicides.

My older brother killed himself by eating pain pills and then putting a plastic bag over his head—just in case. My mother followed a few years later, willing herself out of this world. Cousins, siblings, nephews: dead. Even those who survive often bear the marks or memories of trying.

When someone you love kills himself or herself—and when it happens over and over again, as in my family—suicide becomes as ordinary as crossing the street. It becomes your hand on a glass of milk. It becomes you opening the mail, you going for a walk: see that bridge? See that truck? It becomes the freeway ramp you recall your brother made his first attempt to kill himself, driving the wrong way, desperate for collision. It becomes the plate of food you look at and see your mother, denying herself until she literally starved to death, a gasping skeleton clutching your hand in a bed, so devoid of fluids she could not cry.

When the people you love kill themselves, it becomes a common thing, a normal thing, and an everyday you-could-do-it-too thing. It haunts you. It asks, why not you? What gives you the right to survive?

There is no happy ever after in suicide. No consolation. People 5
die and they are gone. They leave you only with the worst kind of loss,
frozen in time: never-ending guilt and remorse. You are still here and
they will never be again.

But the way they left? It becomes your normal, as easy as following a map: this way out.

My family never believed in heaven. But sometimes I am sure my
brother is visiting me. He says, "Rene's-a-Daisy," which was his childhood nickname for me. He is so real then I can smell him, though his
face floats—as if the afterlife truly has changed him. He has become
as soft as clouds. He tells me to find the other side of sorrow.

Families with suicides all have a story. Ours is one of alcohol-
ism, abuse and mental illness. My brother and I survived childhoods
marked with poverty and molestation. The man we considered our father is a registered predatory sex offender. My brother tried to escape
this history by becoming the king of normal, right on down to the
button-down shirt and pocket protector, as if to hide the fact we came
from squalor. It didn't work. Before he died he said, "I just wanted to
be a good boy."

My mother succumbed to guilt, I believe. What a terrible burden
she carried. She couldn't forgive herself, though she had reason—she
herself was the victim of rape and violence. Her guilt ate at her from
the inside until she could bear it no longer. I wish she were here today,
so I could tell her I forgive her.

In ideal circumstances, death is something we try and outrun our 10
entire lives until we have to sink, relatively gracefully, to its pressures.
Suicide steals all that, from the living and the dead. It is the hole
punched in the picture frame. It is the hole punched in our hearts.

How do you survive? How do you find the other side of sorrow?

I've found hope by helping the living. One of the best decisions

I've ever made was to adopt kids from foster care. My kids bring me joy and redemption and a sense of purpose. Every laugh we share, every touch, is a reminder to me that reality can, indeed, change. The hurt can be soothed, the pain can be seen, and heard. From trauma rises the soul, incandescent and perfect. It was always there, waiting to be embraced.

I also work with men and women facing execution. It might seem that saving the condemned would be a contradiction. But my clients are very similar to my family. No one wants to die. No one chooses to land in this awful place. My clients are in a living nightmare, praying every morning they may awake in a different reality. But every morning they wake in the same cell—just the same as we all do. And we all struggle and go on.

The best way to heal yourself? Heal others.

15   I don't believe we can escape our past. My brother and mother tried it, and it didn't work. We have to make friends with sadness. We have to hold our losses close, and carry them like beloved children. Only when we accept these terrible pains do we realize that the path across is the one that takes us through.

The longer I do this the easier it gets. Isn't it funny, how we can find beauty anywhere? A fallen feather on the ground. An empty nut husk. A child's face, even in hurt or anger—sometimes I think active emotion is the most beautiful thing of all, because it signifies energy.

Joy can be found even in despair. The grey cloud lifts, it moves—it is over there tomorrow; today it may come closer. If we slow ourselves we can find magic in even the deepest sorrow.

Sometimes people argue that one pain is more or less worthy than the other. Nothing could be further from the truth. Pain is not a contest. Pain is universal: it is something we all share. And it is something we can heal in each other.

Someday, I hope I can go for a walk and see a bridge and admire only its curve. I want to see the dimple in a bed and not remember a curved form. I want to see my brother living — that I can never do again — but in the least I want to study his picture and remember his warmth, next to mine, that irreplaceable, precious self, and not remember this: the final exit.

I want to think of everything that came before and will come later,   20
and savor it, breath by precious breath.

What to the Slave
Is the Fourth of July?

Frederick Douglass

Frederick Augustus Washington Bailey (1818–1895) was born into slavery in Maryland. In 1836, he escaped, later taking the last name of "Douglass" to protect his identity. He was a leading abolitionist, celebrated orator, and best-selling author. This speech was delivered in Rochester, New York on July 5, 1852.

Fellow-Citizens — Pardon me, and allow me to ask, why am I called upon to speak here today? What have I, or those I represent, to do with your national independence? Are the great principles of political freedom and of natural justice, embodied in that Declaration of Independence, extended to us? and am I, therefore, called upon to bring our humble offering to the national altar, and to confess the benefits, and express devout gratitude for the blessings, resulting from your independence to us?

Would to God, both for your sakes and ours, that an affirmative answer could be truthfully returned to these questions! Then would my task be light, and my burden easy and delightful. For who is there so cold that a nation's sympathy could not warm him? Who so obdurate and dead to the claims of gratitude, that would not thankfully acknowledge such priceless benefits? Who so stolid and selfish, that would not give his voice to swell the hallelujahs of a nation's jubilee, when the chains of servitude had been torn from his limbs? I am not that man. In a case like that, the dumb might eloquently speak, and the "lame man leap as an hart."

But, such is not the state of the case. I say it with a sad sense of the disparity between us. I am not included within the pale of this glorious anniversary! Your high independence only reveals the immeasurable distance between us. The blessings in which you this day rejoice, are not enjoyed in common. The rich inheritance of justice, liberty, prosperity, and independence, bequeathed by your fathers, is shared by you, not by me. The sunlight that brought life and healing to you, has brought stripes and death to me. This Fourth of July is yours, not mine. You may rejoice, I must mourn. To drag a man in fetters into the grand illuminated temple of liberty, and call upon him to join you in joyous anthems, were inhuman mockery and sacrilegious irony. Do you mean, citizens, to mock me, by asking me to speak today? If so, there is a parallel to your conduct. And let me warn you that it is dangerous to copy the example of a nation whose crimes, towering up to heaven, were thrown down by the breath of the Almighty, burying that nation in irrecoverable ruin! I can today take up the plaintive lament of a peeled and woe-smitten people.

"By the rivers of Babylon, there we sat down. Yea! we wept when we remembered Zion. We hanged our harps upon the willows in the midst thereof. For there, they that carried us away captive, required of us a song; and they who wasted us required of us mirth, saying, Sing us one of the songs of Zion. How can we sing the Lord's song in a strange land? If I forget thee, O Jerusalem, let my right hand forget her cunning. If I do not remember thee, let my tongue cleave to the roof of my mouth."

Fellow-citizens, above your national, tumultuous joy, I hear the mournful wail of millions, whose chains, heavy and grievous yesterday, are today rendered more intolerable by the jubilant shouts that reach them. If I do forget, if I do not faithfully remember those bleeding children of sorrow this day, "may my right hand forget her cunning, 5 and may my tongue cleave to the roof of my mouth!" To forget them, to pass lightly over their wrongs, and to chime in with the popular theme, would be treason most scandalous and shocking, and would make me a reproach before God and the world. My subject, then, fellow-citizens, is American Slavery. I shall see this day and its popular characteristics from the slave's point of view. Standing there, identified with the American bondman, making his wrongs mine, I do not hesitate to declare, with all my soul, that the character and conduct of this nation never looked blacker to me than on this Fourth of July. Whether we turn to the declarations of the past, or to the professions of the present, the conduct of the nation seems equally hideous and revolting. America is false to the past, false to the present, and solemnly binds herself to be false to the future. Standing with God and the crushed and bleeding slave on this occasion, I will, in the name of humanity which is outraged, in the name of liberty which is fettered, in the name of the constitution and the bible, which are disregarded and trampled upon, dare to call in question and to denounce, with all the emphasis I can command, everything that serves to perpetuate slavery—the great sin and shame of America! "I will not equivocate; I will not excuse;" I will use the severest language I can command; and yet not one word shall escape me that any man, whose judgment is not blinded by prejudice, or who is not at heart a slaveholder, shall not confess to be right and just.

But I fancy I hear some one of my audience say, it is just in this circumstance that you and your brother abolitionists fail to make a favorable impression on the public mind. Would you argue more, and denounce less, would you persuade more and rebuke less, your cause would be much more likely to succeed. But, I submit, where all is plain there is nothing to be argued. What point in the anti-slavery creed would you have me argue? On what branch of the subject do the people of this country need light? Must I undertake to prove that the slave is a man? That point is conceded already. Nobody doubts it. The slaveholders themselves acknowledge it in the enactment of laws for their government. They acknowledge it when they punish disobedience on the part of the slave. There are seventy-two crimes in the state of Virginia, which, if committed by a black man (no matter how ignorant he be), subject him to the punishment of death; while only two of these same crimes will subject a white man to the like punishment. What is this but the acknowledgment that the slave is a moral, intellectual, and responsible being. The manhood of the slave is conceded. It is admitted in the fact that southern statute books are covered with enactments forbidding, under severe fines and penalties, the teaching of the slave to read or write. When you can point to any such laws, in reference to the beasts of the field, then I may consent to argue the manhood of the slave. When the dogs in your streets, when the fowls of the air, when the cattle on your hills, when the fish of the sea, and the reptiles that crawl, shall be unable to distinguish the slave from a brute, then will I argue with you that the slave is a man!

For the present, it is enough to affirm the equal manhood of the Negro race. Is it not astonishing that, while we are plowing, planting, and reaping, using all kinds of mechanical tools, erecting houses, constructing bridges, building ships, working in metals of brass, iron, copper, silver, and gold; that, while we are reading, writing, and cyphering, acting as clerks, merchants, and secretaries, having among us lawyers, doctors, ministers, poets, authors, editors, orators, and teachers; that, while we are engaged in all manner of enterprises common to other men — digging gold in California, capturing the whale in the Pacific, feeding sheep and cattle on the hillside, living, moving, acting, thinking, planning, living in families as husbands, wives, and children, and, above all, confessing and worshiping the Christian's God, and looking hopefully for life and immortality beyond the grave—we are called upon to prove that we are men!

Would you have me argue that man is entitled to liberty? that he is the rightful owner of his own body? You have already declared it. Must I argue the wrongfulness of slavery? Is that a question for republicans? Is it to be settled by the rules of logic and argumentation, as a matter beset with great difficulty, involving a doubtful application of the principle of justice, hard to be understood? How should I look today in the presence of Americans, dividing and subdividing a discourse, to show that men have a natural right to freedom, speaking of it relatively and positively, negatively and affirmatively? To do so, would be to make myself ridiculous, and to offer an insult to your understanding. There is not a man beneath the canopy of heaven that does not know that slavery is wrong for him.

What! am I to argue that it is wrong to make men brutes, to rob them of their liberty, to work them without wages, to keep them ignorant of their relations to their fellow-men, to beat them with sticks, to flay their flesh with the lash, to load their limbs with irons, to hunt them with dogs, to sell them at auction, to sunder their families, to knock out their teeth, to burn their flesh, to starve them into obedience and submission to their masters? Must I argue that a system, thus marked with blood and stained with pollution, is wrong? No; I will not. I have better employment for my time and strength than such arguments would imply.

10   What, then, remains to be argued? Is it that slavery is not divine; that God did not establish it; that our doctors of divinity are mistaken? There is blasphemy in the thought. That which is inhuman cannot be divine. Who can reason on such a proposition! They that can, may! I cannot. The time for such argument is past.

At a time like this, scorching irony, not convincing argument, is needed. Oh! had I the ability, and could I reach the nation's ear, I would today pour out a fiery stream of biting ridicule, blasting reproach, withering sarcasm, and stern rebuke. For it is not light that is needed, but fire; it is not the gentle shower, but thunder. We need the storm, the whirlwind, and the earthquake. The feeling of the nation must be quickened; the conscience of the nation must be roused; the propriety of the nation must be startled; the hypocrisy of the nation must be exposed; and its crimes against God and man must be proclaimed and denounced.

What to the American slave is your Fourth of July? I answer, a day that reveals to him, more than all other days in the year, the gross injustice and cruelty to which he is the constant victim. To him, your celebration is a sham; your boasted liberty, an unholy license; your national greatness, swelling vanity; your sounds of rejoicing are empty and heartless; your denunciations of tyrants, brass-fronted impudence; your shouts of liberty and equality, hollow mockery; your prayers and hymns, your sermons and thanksgivings, with all your religious parade and solemnity, are to him mere bombast, fraud, deception, impiety, and hypocrisy—a thin veil to cover up crimes which would disgrace a nation of savages. There is not a nation on the earth guilty of practices more shocking and bloody, than are the people of these United States, at this very hour.

Go where you may, search where you will, roam through all the monarchies and despotisms of the old world, travel through South America, search out every abuse, and when you have found the last, lay your facts by the side of the every-day practices of this nation, and you will say with me, that, for revolting barbarity and shameless hypocrisy, America reigns without a rival.

The Crime of Removal

Ralph Waldo Emerson

Ralph Waldo Emerson (1803–1882) was an essayist, philosopher, and poet known for his central role in the development of transcendentalism, a religious and philosophical movement popular in the US during the 1820s and 1830s. In 1836, Emerson wrote to President Martin Van Buren to protest the government's removal of the Cherokees from their land.

To Martin Van Buren, President of the United States
Concord, Mass., April 23, 1838.

Sir: The seat you fill places you in a relation of credit and nearness to every citizen. By right and natural position, every citizen is your friend. Before any acts contrary to his own judgment or interest have repelled the affections of any man, each may look with trust and living anticipation to your government. Each has the highest right to call your attention to such subjects as are of a public nature, and properly belong to the chief magistrate; and the good magistrate will feel a joy in meeting such confidence. In this belief and at the instance of a few of my friends and neighbors, I crave of your patience a short hearing for their sentiments and my own: and the circumstance that my name will be utterly unknown to you will only give the fairer chance to your equitable construction of what I have to say.

Sir, my communication respects the sinister rumors that fill this part of the country concerning the Cherokee people. The interest always felt in the aboriginal population—an interest naturally growing as that decays—has been heightened in regard to this tribe. Even in our distant State some good rumor of their worth and civility has ar-

rived. We have learned with joy their improvement in the social arts.
We have read their newspapers. We have seen some of them in our
schools and colleges. In common with the great body of the American
people, we have witnessed with sympathy the painful labors of these
red men to redeem their own race from the doom of eternal inferiori-
ty, and to borrow and domesticate in the tribe the arts and customs of
the Caucasian race. And notwithstanding the unaccountable apathy
with which of late years the Indians have been sometimes abandoned
to their enemies, it is not to be doubted that it is the good pleasure
and the understanding of all humane persons in the Republic, of the
men and the matrons sitting in the thriving independent families all
over the land, that they shall be duly cared for; that they shall taste
justice and love from all to whom we have delegated the office of
dealing with them.

The newspapers now inform us that, in December, 1835, a treaty   5
contracting for the exchange of all the Cherokee territory was pre-
tended to be made by an agent on the part of the United States with
some persons appearing on the part of the Cherokees; that the fact afterwards transpired that these deputies did by no means represent the
will of the nation; and that, out of eighteen thousand souls compos-
ing the nation, fifteen thousand six hundred and sixty-eight have pro-
tested against the so-called treaty. It now appears that the government
of the United States choose to hold the Cherokees to this sham treaty,
and are proceeding to execute the same. Almost the entire Cherokee
Nation stand up and say, "This is not our act. Behold us. Here are we.
Do not mistake that handful of deserters for us;" and the American
President and the Cabinet, the Senate and the House of Representatives, neither hear these men nor see them, and are contracting to put
this active nation into carts and boats, and to drag them over mountains and rivers to a wilderness at a vast distance beyond the Missis-

sippi. And a paper purporting to be an army order fixes a month from this day as the hour for this doleful removal.

In the name of God, sir, we ask you if this be so. Do the newspapers rightly inform us? Men and women with pale and perplexed faces meet one another in the streets and churches here, and ask if this be so. We have inquired if this be a gross misrepresentation from the party opposed to the government and anxious to blacken it with the people. We have looked in the newspapers of different parties and find a horrid confirmation of the tale. We are slow to believe it. We hoped the Indians were misinformed, and that their remonstrance was premature, and will turn out to be a needless act of terror.

The piety, the principle that is left in the United States, if only in its coarsest form, a regard to the speech of men, — forbid us to entertain it as a fact. Such a dereliction of all faith and virtue, such a denial of justice, and such deafness to screams for mercy were never heard of in times of peace and in the dealing of a nation with its own allies and wards, since the earth was made. Sir, does this government think that the people of the United States are become savage and mad? From their mind are the sentiments of love and a good nature wiped clean out? The soul of man, the justice, the mercy that is the heart's heart in all men, from Maine to Georgia, does abhor this business.

In speaking thus the sentiments of my neighbors and my own, perhaps I overstep the bounds of decorum. But would it not be a higher indecorum coldly to argue a matter like this? We only state the fact that a crime is projected that confounds our understandings by its magnitude, — a crime that really deprives us as well as the Cherokees of a country — for how could we call the conspiracy that should crush these poor Indians our government, or the land that was cursed by their parting and dying imprecations our country, any more? You, sir, will bring down that renowned chair in which you sit into infamy if your seal is set to this instrument of perfidy; and the name of this nation, hitherto the sweet omen of religion and liberty, will stink to the world.

You will not do us the injustice of connecting this remonstrance with any sectional and party feeling. It is in our hearts the simplest commandment of brotherly love. We will not have this great and solemn claim upon national and human justice huddled aside under the flimsy plea of its being a party act. Sir, to us the questions upon which the government and the people have been agitated during the past year, touching the prostration of the currency and of trade, seem but motes in comparison. These hard times, it is true, have brought the discussion home to every farmhouse and poor man's house in this town; but it is the chirping of grasshoppers beside the immortal question whether justice shall be done by the race of civilized to the race of savage man,—whether all the attributes of reason, of civility, of justice, and even of mercy, shall be put off by the American people, and so vast an outrage upon the Cherokee Nation and upon human nature shall be consummated.

One circumstance lessens the reluctance with which I intrude at this time on your attention my conviction that the government ought to be admonished of a new historical fact, which the discussion of this question has disclosed, namely, that there exists in a great part of the Northern people a gloomy diffidence in the moral character of the government.

On the broaching of this question, a general expression of despondency, of disbelief that any good will accrue from a remonstrance on an act of fraud and robbery, appeared in those men to whom we naturally turn for aid and counsel. Will the American government steal? Will it lie? Will it kill?—We ask triumphantly. Our counsellors and old statesmen here say that ten years ago they would have staked their lives on the affirmation that the proposed Indian measures could not be executed; that the unanimous country would put them down. And now the steps of this crime follow each other so fast, at such fatally quick time, that the millions of virtuous citizens, whose agents the government are, have no place to interpose, and must shut their eyes until the last howl and wailing of these tormented villages and tribes shall afflict the ear of the world.

I will not hide from you, as an indication of the alarming distrust, that a letter addressed as mine is, and suggesting to the mind of the Executive the plain obligations of man, has a burlesque character in the apprehensions of some of my friends. I, sir, will not beforehand treat you with the contumely of this distrust. I will at least state to you this fact, and show you how plain and humane people, whose love would be honor, regard the policy of the government, and what injurious inferences they draw as to the minds of the governors. A man with your experience in affairs must have seen cause to appreciate the futility of opposition to the moral sentiment. However feeble the sufferer and however great the oppressor, it is in the nature of things that the blow should recoil upon the aggressor. For God is in the sentiment, and it cannot be withstood. The potentate and the people perish before it; but with it, and as its executor, they are omnipotent.

I write thus, sir, to inform you of the state of mind these Indian tidings have awakened here, and to pray with one voice more that you, whose hands are strong with the delegated power of fifteen millions of men, will avert with that might the terrific injury which threatens the Cherokee tribe.

With great respect, sir, I am your fellow citizen,
Ralph Waldo Emerson.

An Open Letter to Medical Students

Down Syndrome, Paradox, and Medicine

George Estreich

George Estreich is an Oregon poet and writer who has written extensively about medical and disability issues. The Shape of the Eye, *his book about his second daughter, Laura, who has Down syndrome, won the 2012 Oregon Book Award for Creative Nonfiction. "An Open Letter" attempts to share "questions and insights" about Down syndrome, especially to future doctors.*

If you're reading this, you could be anyone—a bioethicist, a Facebook friend, an adult with Down syndrome—but the "you" I have in mind is a future clinician. As a writer and parent of someone with Down syndrome, my aim is to share questions and insights that may be useful to you. Clinical encounters involving people with intellectual disabilities can be both charged and complex; understanding the complexities may help improve the encounters, by helping clinicians see the patient more clearly. I will focus on Down syndrome, because it's what I know best, but ultimately I wish to emphasize similarities between people with Down syndrome, people with other disabilities, and those of us who, because we lack named conditions, are presumed to be "normal."

At this point, you may be expecting to be scolded or inspired. In the first case, I would recount an anecdote involving an insensitive physician and warn you against analogous behavior, perhaps cautioning you against language offensive to people with disabilities. In the second, I would offer an appealing, positive story about my daughter, thus inspiring you to recognize her essential humanity, to see her as a person and not as a diagnosis.

These are common scripts, and they have their uses. Still, I try to avoid them. Practically speaking, no one was ever scolded into enlightenment, and what we call "inspiration" is often weaponized sentiment, a battering ram with a Positive Message printed on the end. Although I've written a book[1] about my daughter, the humanity and value of people with Down syndrome—and of people with other disabilities, however defined—is a starting point for me, not a persuasive destination. One should not need an inspiring story to be valued.

I wrote the book about my daughter for many reasons, but one was that since the attention she drew was inevitable, I might as well work with it. If people were going to stare, I might as well lend some depth to the picture; because, as I found, they were often staring at a projection. This projection—call it a huggable ghost—was a vague shape, a diagnosis with a personality, a mix of sweetness and tragedy, of angels and heart defects and maternal age. It was a way of imagining Down syndrome, but it hid the individual. The projection, the ghost, obscured the child.

5   In that book, my project was to restore the child to view. In this letter, my project is to help banish the ghost from the exam room. To that end, I want to discuss some of the obstacles to seeing people with Down syndrome clearly and on their terms, and to suggest a paradox: since one of the greatest of those obstacles is the medical description of the condition, a thoughtful physician will need to both absorb that descriptive knowledge and be able to set it aside.

No one says that people with lung cancer have a particular personality, but the idea that there is a "Down syndrome personality" (sweet, affectionate, cheerful) is, in my experience, common among clinicians. It's less common among parents, but even when asserted, it's usually to support an individual story, and not an idea of diagnostic sameness. Parents are intensely aware of a child's distinct personality and situated life, her story in time.

The tendency to equate diagnosis with personality has roots in medical history, and ultimately in the history of Western thinking about race. The condition now known as Down syndrome was first described in Western medicine in 1866, by the young physician John Langdon Down, then medical superintendent of the Royal Earlswood Asylum for Idiots[2]. When Down christened the condition "Mongolian idiocy," believing the "idiots" in his care to have descended a hierarchy of races in utero, he grafted ideas of race onto ideas of disability. It was a brilliant error, a stroke of blurry insight: the list form could incorporate both observable features and presumed ethnic characteristics. Down was no simple racist, and in his treatment of asylum residents, he was ahead of his time[3]. But he saw the individuals under his care through the lens of group attributes.

For this reason, the claim that people with Down syndrome are "sweet," however well intentioned, makes me uneasy. It feeds the perception that Down syndrome is the "good" special need, the appealing one, which seems unfair to kids with behavioral difficulties. It can also misfire in any number of ways: children with Down syndrome who are expected to be sweet but aren't can be seen as disappointments; children with Down syndrome are often expected to give hugs to strangers, a real problem given the high rates of sexual abuse committed against women with intellectual disabilities[4]; children with Down syndrome can be seen mainly in terms of static behavioral qualities and not in terms of what they might learn.

But most of all, "sweet" is something you say of a child. People with Down syndrome now have a life expectancy of around 60[5]. If we think of them as permanent children, we will be less able to imagine a place for them in the world as adults.

10   There are few certainties with Down syndrome. Because we know where it begins (with a nondisjunction, or a failure of a chromosome pair to separate during cell division) and what results (an infant with a suite of typical features), we can believe, too easily, that it is known. But the condition is incredibly variable, and those variations, entering a changing world, result in many different outcomes.

Ironically, among all the probabilities, possibilities, and distant chances associated with Down syndrome, the primary certainty—what used to be called "retardation"—is not clearly within the domain of medicine. To have an atrioventricular canal defect, or leukemia, is one thing. But to be less able than most to manipulate information, to reason abstractly, is another. It's not only that people with Down syndrome have a range of abilities, which overlaps with the range considered "normal." It's that ability itself cannot be measured or considered outside of social context.

Even setting aside the long history of underestimating what people with Down syndrome can do, it's worth noting that people with intellectual disabilities, besides being among the most despised minorities in our culture, are cast in a harsh light by a society that prizes intellectual ability and accomplishment. Negotiating our text-heavy, Information Age democracy requires an unprecedented degree of literacy and technological ability. In work, in education, those abilities are heavily incentivized. Indeed, our educational system encourages us to equate intellectual performance with self-worth, to motivate ourselves by seeing ourselves as our grades and accomplishments. Teaching English at the university level, I've seen this in many of my students—and in myself, too, a lesson I've learned too deeply to forget.

Which brings me back to you, reader. You don't get into medical school without taking ability itself—and particularly intellectual ability—seriously. The entire project assumes capabilities that tend to be diminished in people with Down syndrome: skill with language and numbers, ease with abstraction, the ability to process, retain, and manipulate large quantities of information.

A question, then, is how to imagine the value of people who don't have those abilities: how to value your own achievement without devaluing those for whom those achievements are difficult or impossible. Much in our culture, from ubiquitous insults based on intelligence to the medical definitions of normalcy to the relative invisibility of people with disabilities, teaches us separation. Clinical encounters tend to take place across a gulf, a chasm both narrow and deep. The question is how to step across it.

The divide between doctor and intellectually disabled patient can   15
be framed as a divide between able and disabled. But I think it is best seen in terms of interpretive power.

To be intellectually disabled is to have your life be synonymous with an opinion not worth listening to: on Facebook, in every comment section, in conversation, that's what the words idiot, moron, and retard imply. Conversely, being a clinician confers authority: your words matter, weighted not only by study, experience, and your resulting expertise, or by the prestige accorded the profession, but also by the white coat, the stethoscope, the successive human barriers (e.g., receptionist, nurse) that frame an appointment, the ritual of gates dividing you from the patient.

You have, in other words, power to declare meaning. Paradoxically enough, your best course may be to refrain from using it. That is, apart from treating a given patient with Down syndrome like any other, the power to declare meaning entails not pronouncing what a patient is or what her life means, but instead learning to listen.

From the moment a child is diagnosed with a disability, her parents are swamped with interpretations, advice, and predicted futures. But predictions and interpretations, even comforting ones, may be less useful than an honest uncertainty. For any child, the agents of nurture—parents, clinicians, therapists, educators—are there to help keep her future as open as possible. That way, the child, when she is ready (when she is no longer a patient, no longer a child) can begin to find her own way, and to choose the meanings for herself.

End Notes

1. Estreich G. *The Shape of the Eye*. New York, NY: Tarcher Penguin, 2013.

2. Down JL. Observations on an Ethnic Classification of Idiots. 1866. *Clinical Lectures and Reports by the Medical and Surgical Staff of the London Hospital*, vol 3, 259262.

3. Ward OC. *John Langdon Down*, 1828-1896: A Caring Pioneer. London, UK: Royal Society of Medicine Press, 1998.

4. Wissink IB, van Vugt E, Moonen X, Stams GJ, Hendriks J. Sexual Abuse Involving Children With An Intellectual Disability: A Narrative Review. *Res Dev Disabil.* 2015, 36: 20-35.

5. Bittles AH, Glasson EJ. Clinical, Social, And Ethical Implications Of Changing Life Expectancy In Down Syndrome. *Dev Med Child Neurol.* 2004, 46(4): 282-286.

Running Mountains

Jenny Forrester

Jenny Forrester grew up in rural Colorado, and now lives in Portland, Oregon, where she curates and hosts Unchaste Readers, *a long-running monthly reading series by women. This selection comes from her 2017 memoir* Narrow River, Wide Sky.

Mean Patty, sometimes my best friend, said, "you got to state cuz no body else in this school wants to run distance and all you do is move your feet slow like this for a mile or two and you win."

I'd qualified for the state track meet, having come in first at the district level.

She slow-motion ran down the hallway, keeping her hands limp like I did when I ran because it kept my shoulders from tightening up. It did look slow.

Cowboy Justin, a football player, snort-laughed, which was funny by itself, and then said, "She does look like that when she gets tired."

Math-smart Tim, with a mean alcoholic father, said, "She's fast, 5 you know. Fast as an Indian."

Patty said, "Shhheeeez, like it's hard to beat a bunch of drunks," and then smiled at Tim. I wished she were ugly then, but she wasn't, and she could say whatever she wanted for a laugh and be mean enough that everyone feared her. Tim's family fostered American Indian children. Claudina stood beside Patty and laughed to hurt me. She was Navajo, a foster child, and Patty's friend for the day. Patty could make us turn against each other and ourselves.

Patty and Tim were rancher royalty, like pioneer royalty, three generations on and could say anything they wanted and no one argued. They all claimed pioneer blood and American Indian blood through a great-great-grandmother so they could be on all sides of a rural argument. Tim once took me out to his truck to show me a fawn he'd skinned, to impress me, he said. He'd give me the hide. "It'll be soft," he said. I cried, though. He stood silent beside me, pulled the tarp back over the fawn. An angry gray wave. "Thought you'd like it," he growled.

Patty was probably right about me not having to run very fast, but not because of the color of a runner's skin like she said, but because there wasn't much competition — very few kids wanted to run distance. I turned to my locker and heard the crackle of static in my hair. Perfect timing.

I heard laughter and Patty said, "Maybe that static makes you faster at going in circles."

10   Mom said I won because of God. She wanted me to be humble, "God is generous with you. Always remember that winning is God's glory, not yours," she said whenever I won or placed well at a meet, but my failures were my own. Mom's religion, like her temperament and her affection, ebbed and flowed. A tide in a high desert on the reservation or an avalanche in a mountain town. We traveled hours to track meets in the Four Corners area. During track season, our lives rose higher and felt hotter and colder. The chance of a college scholarship if it was God's plan.

The Oreos in my pack were there for the ride back, three hundred miles.

"It'll be a reward," Mom said, because she rarely bought junk food.

She said, "Don't eat them until after. You know how you get." I couldn't stop once I started, my own uncontrollable tide.

She packed them into the backpack, kissed me on the crown of the head, and said, "You can do anything you put your mind to."

She hugged me and said, "You're as fast as an Indian, just remem- 15
ber that." That comparison gave me strength and fueled my desire to
belong, my desire for many kin, and lasted just long enough until I
turned soft again and knew I didn't belong.

I felt deep pressure for this track meet. We got a town send-
off—dozens of people gathered around the rented van, driven by Mr.
Willburn, sweeter than Mr. Adcock. He'd drive us through the state of
Colorado to get there, from one corner to the other, north then east
across the divide.

As we left, a man said, "You better bring a medal home, little girl."

Mom said, "You be gracious. It's not all about you, and for goodness' sake don't cry," when I told her that I was afraid of letting everyone down.

Alone in a motel room in Denver—I was the only girl to make it
to the state meet—I held my cleats to my chest, Tammy's shoes. She
was the daughter of the town journalist. The shoes had a sort of magic
because Tammy shared them with others—so many of us couldn't
afford our own. We applied our successes to them, feeling mightier
instead of poorer. I changed to short spikes for the fancy rubberized
track. Mancos High School didn't have a track. For a 400-meter run,
we ran about one and a half times around the football field in a well-
worn path.

I focused on the shoes so I could ignore the Oreos. 20

I prayed, "Please God, let me win a medal. Please God."

I prayed and fell asleep and dreamed that the Sleeping Ute Mountain on the Ute Mountain Reservation, southeast of Cortez, had risen
according to the legend we'd learned on the playground, to kill all the
white people. Patty drove a pioneer wagon, whipping the four horses
of the apocalypse, in Biblical colors—red, black, white, and pale, but

she didn't see the Walking Ute Mountain comoing up behind her, walking toward her. I thought it was funny until I heard God yell and I woke up to the alarm.

Before I left the room, I noticed the painting above my bed. An American Indian rode a painted pony, both of them, heads bent and leaning into the wind, the sky in the painting was lightning and shades of red in the distance.

I cried until the coach banged on the door and said, "It's time."

25 God and I got a third-place medal in the 2-mile that day.

I offered the Oreos to the boys in the van, but they had plenty of their own food. I ate the cookies and wanted more.

Later, when the school year ended, I walked out of the trailer on a June day, still thin from track season.

I wore a bikini—navy blue with tiny white polka dots—first time I'd ever worn a bikini.

Mom worked the garden, chucking rocks over the barbed wire.

30 I'd had another bad night. Bored and lonely while Mom worked her waitressing job at the Millwood Junction, I'd tried to make cookies without butter or eggs or banana or oil. I used milk and flour.

"Thanks for trying," Brian said. "For cookies without butter or eggs, they're really good," but he didn't eat any.

Mom looked up at me, "You've gained a couple of pounds." I put my hands to my belly, trying to cover it.

She was right. That morning, the scale said that I weighed ninety-two pounds. Not too skinny for a five-foot-two inch girl, but thin enough, especially for someone who used to be chubby and who would be chubby again, more than chubby.

"Yeah, I guess," I said.

35 "Yeah, I guess," she repeated, her tone sarcasm and daggers.

She fit that label "normal." She didn't have the battle I had with my expanding, shrinking, expanding body.

Maybe she was mad because I used up the milk she'd been saving for our meals.

Maybe she was mad because she'd spent money on a bikini only to see me with a puffy stomach.

Maybe she was mad because she couldn't decide whether it was better for us to be hungry and me to be thin enough to pass for normal or better for us to have enough food and me blimp up and float away, but my weight didn't reflect whether we had money or not.

Next day, she told me I couldn't wear my favorite sweater—too tight, try something looser.

Brian told me not to drink water when I was thirsty. It would make me weaker and thirstier. He told me to drink water when I was eating to fill me up.

He told me to eat things in a different order and a different way so that I wouldn't be so hungry.

During track season, he told me not to drink water when I ran, and not right after because I'd just want more water. I'd start to need it more.

"You gotta need less. If you give yourself less, you'll need less. You'll be tougher."

A stack of diet books and exercise tapes sat piled on Mom's nightstand that was also the coffee table where she slept in the living room—Richard Simmons, Weight Watchers, aerobics with Jane Fonda, her public image redeemed after protesting against the Vietnam War, and there was Helen Gurley Brown and a pile of Cosmo magazines.

Brian said Mom's butt was too big, but to me, she was tiny except for the soft belly where my brother and I had been.

I wrote in my diary, "I feel depressed about my weight—do

something!" and "God gives me everything and what do I do?"

Brian, Mom, and the rest of our extended family poked fun at my fat, my constant battle with fat, my belly, my sometimes round belly.

My flesh, a universe, I said, "I expand and contract," to make people laugh, to divert them from criticizing my weight. There was safety in the solitude of excess flesh, and there was comfort in food. I watched the sun in its vast arc, as thunderclouds gathered and the lightning flashed across the world. I hungered to understand. I wanted to fill that hunger and the other hunger that would be a sin to feed, and I fed it with food because it was all I could think to do. In that small town in the middle of an expanse between one place and somewhere else, there wasn't much to do. I wanted my mother to understand my hunger, but I couldn't understand it either.

50   My breasts grew large even when I was thin. I joked about my breasts, laughing before others, putting people at ease with judgment, theirs and my own.

Mom said, "I hope you take this the right way. I bought you a shirt." It said, "Flat is beautiful." We laughed at the word stretched across my breasts.

Every track season, I had that five pounds, that ten pounds, to lose for running long distances.

"You have heart," my coach said, "It makes up for what you don't have."

Mom said, "You need a support bra," and she let me know about the expense. "You have to be modest."

55   Mondays I started new diets, which meant feeling hungry as much as possible because weight loss only happened through hunger. I ignored the dizziness with small rituals—writing food lists, weighing myself, counting to distract myself: 1, 2, 3, 4, 4, 3, 2, 1, 1, 2, 3, 3, 2, 1, 2, 2, 1, 1, etc.

Mom told me her mother was bone thin when she died. When she told me this, she looked off into the sky, the blue of her eyes remained dry. She held her emotions in check for our sake as often as she could. She believed adult sadness upset children too much and so should be contained.

"People said that she looked so good because she was thin," Mom said. "But she was dying—people become thin while they're dying. She'd been curvier and rounder during most of her life. You're more like her than I am."

Mom paused, "Do you understand what that means?" Unsure, I said "Yes."

"You do? What does it mean?"

"Um . . ."   60

"No, you don't understand. You can't understand. It means people thought it was more important that she be thin than that she live."

"Yeah. So, it doesn't matter what you weigh," I said, hopeful and excited, thinking I understood.

"Well," she said, "that's not exactly what I meant. You're like her. You look like her, and you're busty like her." I sensed an edge. Some thought or fear I didn't want to touch.

She turned to the mirror, adjusted her long denim skirt, belted over a sweater. "Do you think this makes me look—well, too bunchy?"

"You could never look bunchy," I said. She smiled.   65

I sat on my bed ashamed, bunchy, busty, and too much. And still I wanted more. I always wanted more.

I Spent the Last 15 Years Trying to Become an American

William Han

William Han was born in New Zealand. He graduated from Yale University and Columbia University Law School, and practiced law in New York City. He lists his current location as "TBD" (to be determined). His essay first appeared in Vox *(www.vox.com) in June 2015 and describes his experiences with the difficult bureaucracy of US immigration law.*

I have lived in America for the past 15 years. I have two Ivy League degrees. And I am on the verge of deportation.

Despite being an "honorary American," as I have often jokingly introduced myself, I am in fact a citizen of New Zealand. I was 18 years old when I first came to America. I still remember the excitement I felt when, very late at night, my flight from Auckland touched down at JFK. Americans may romanticize New Zealand for its natural beauty, for being Middle Earth, but we from the small country often dreamed of the metropolis, longed for its culture, its opportunities, its sense of being the center of the world. And I was about to be a part of all that.

I had come to America to attend Yale. Barbara Bush, President Bush's daughter, turned out to be in my class. I spent four dutiful years there and graduated with honors, initially majoring in math and physics before switching to the humanities. (Later I would from time to time regret this decision, as immigration rules are somewhat more lenient when you have a degree in "STEM"—science, technology, engineering, and mathematics—although even with STEM graduates the immigration system is badly dysfunctional.)

I then decided to go to law school at Columbia. I was lucky enough to get cushy jobs at prestigious law firms despite the Great Recession, and to work on high-profile cases representing Fortune 500 companies.

All of these years I have spent in America, I have spent legally. 5
I have been determined to do everything on the up and up. From college to law school to professional life, from student visa to work visa, I have scrupulously followed every immigration regulation, paid all my taxes, filed all the papers I had to file, and have not so much as received a parking ticket.

But it turns out that following all the rules is not enough. A move into public interest work unexpectedly fell through, leading to the imminent cancellation of my work visa. Come July, my current visa will expire, and — again in the spirit of obeying the rules — I will get on a plane to somewhere else in the world, anywhere but America. Following all of Uncle Sam's rules has led me, 15 years down the road, to a plane ticket booked on short notice to anywhere but here. Maybe at some point in the indefinite future I will be able to come back, but I cannot count on it, certainly not the when or the how. Maybe in five years, maybe 10, maybe never.

I have done battle with the US immigration system for a decade and half, and I have lost. And here's what I've learned along the way.

I like it here. Americans are such decent, well-meaning people. You may be surprised to hear this, but Americans as people have been more welcoming to me than people most anywhere else. Indeed, of the four countries I have lived in, including the one where I was born and the one where I spent my formative years, America has come to feel more like home to me than anywhere else. My mother says I have converted to the "American religion." And my early expectations have not been disappointed: What I do in America, in the metropolis, seems far more likely to matter, to have an impact in the world, than anything I may do elsewhere. When I studied math and physics in college, I studied with world-renowned scholars. When I worked at law firms, I worked with some of the world's most important corporations.

Numerous American friends, when the subject of my immigration status came up, have said to me things to the effect of, "Why don't you just become a citizen?" To the Americans I have known, it really seems that people, or at least law-abiding people like me, should be able to just go down to the DMV, fill out some paperwork, and get citizenship. Time and again I have had to disabuse my friends of this misconception. What matters when it comes to obtaining citizenship is your "status" while you're in America, and your status can be difficult to change. Years spent as a student do not count. Neither do years on a work visa unless your employer is willing to sponsor your green card. Marrying an American works, as a thousand films and television shows have taught us, because it allows a change of status to permanent resident. But if you wish to follow the rules, as I do, then it must be a bona fide marriage. And if you take important personal decisions such as marriage seriously, then you may not wish to have their timing dictated by Homeland Security.

10   Right now there is no viable path for me to gain citizenship or even to stay in this country, because right now there is no way for me to get a green card. I cannot obtain employer sponsorship. My parents did not have the foresight to have obtained earlier US citizenships for themselves. And now is not the right time for marriage.

American immigration law leaves the skilled immigrant feeling like an indentured serf.

At every step, the immigration system sets up roadblocks for the law-abiding immigrant. An employer who wishes to hire an immigrant employee has to sponsor a work visa and bear the application cost and lawyer's fees; federal regulations bar the employee from paying those costs on behalf of the employer. Even if an employer is willing to incur the costs of sponsoring the employee's work visa, it is more likely than not that the employee will fail to obtain the visa, because the number of work visas given out every year is capped at a level far below the number of applicants. This year, 233,000 highly skilled applicants filed for work visas, but by law the government could only allow 85,000 of them to have visas, 20,000 of those being reserved for applicants with advanced degrees. The rest are turned away, even though they are certified to be skilled, with many holding US degrees, and even though American businesses have indicated that they need these applicants.

Finally, the federal government hands out these visas in October of each year when the federal fiscal year begins, but it accepts applications up to six months in advance, which means that to have any chance of receiving a visa, a skilled foreigner needs to apply in early April. That means that this applicant needs to convince an American employer to offer him or her a job by April without expecting any actual work until October, bear the costs of applying for the visa, and still live with the likelihood that the government may not issue the visa anyway. By any measure, this is a tall order. In my experience, most employers simply (and very reasonably) throw up their hands and say they don't want all this hassle.

Additionally, an H1-B visa (the most common form of work visa and the only form available to most) is only valid for three years and renewable only once. This means that the skilled legal immigrant must obtain permanent residency or a green card if he or she wishes to stay for more than a few years. Again, an employer can sponsor an employee's green card, but the employer must again bear the costs, which can run to the tens of thousands of dollars, and again the employee cannot offer to pay the cost. Employers are often reluctant to engage in this kind of sponsorship because of the cost and because there is no guarantee that the employee in question would stay at the organization after obtaining the green card, and there is also no guarantee that the employer will even want the employee to stay.

15   Where I have worked, I would bring up the green card possibility as tactfully as I knew how, only to be told that the higher-ups needed to discuss the matter. I would bring up the issue again a few months later, only to be told again that there needed to be a discussion. Eventually, a senior partner told me that the firm simply would not sponsor my green card, no matter what happened, and that I should stop asking. In the end, seeing that I was unlikely to obtain a green card in the corporate world anyway, I opted for altruism and public interest work, only to have that decision not work out—this is how much risk a job change can entail for an immigrant.

I don't want to give the impression that I begrudge my employers; they merely reacted to the system they faced in a way that was reasonable from their perspective. And at least some of my bosses went to bat for me and lobbied their fellow higher-ups to help me out; it is only unfortunate that they were unsuccessful.

American immigration law leaves the skilled immigrant feeling like an indentured serf. At every turn, I've had to rely on my employer for sponsorship, whether it be for a work visa or a green card. An immigrant who quits while an application is pending necessarily loses that sponsorship, even if the application may remain pending for years at a time in the case of green cards. And any work visa holder who quits or is terminated from a job without immediately finding a new employer who is willing to take on all the trouble of hiring an immigrant quickly loses the visa and is required to leave America.

I have experienced these fears and frustrations. They leave you feeling like your life is not your own, that you are not living life at all but rather living a series of arbitrary immigration rules. If you feel that your time and energy can genuinely be better spent on something other than your current job, too bad; you will stick to this suboptimal work anyway, just because the risk of leaping to something else is too great. If you feel a desperate need to take time off to recharge your batteries, then don't expect to be able to come back. If your employer does something that truly troubles you, your American colleagues may resign on principle, New Republic style, but you have not the luxury of principles.

Employers who hire immigrant workers have to certify to the Labor Department that the immigrants and their American co-workers in similar positions work under similar conditions and receive similar pay. But nonetheless, the work visa gives the employer all the leverage in the employment relationship—an employee who cannot risk changing jobs can hardly bargain for much.

Another problem with the employer-dependent immigration system: visa holders are barred from founding and working on startups. Immigrants on work visas are legally only allowed to work for the organizations currently sponsoring their visas; if they devote their after-work hours to some Silicon Valley-style side project that may turn into the next Apple or Google, then they're breaking the law.

My friends say I am precisely the kind of immigrant whom the United States should wish to retain. My friends are kind people, and I am no Albert Einstein or Steve Jobs. But at the risk of being immodest, I should say that my American friends are right on this particular point. I am well-educated. I have contributed economically and otherwise to this country, which I love with the zeal of a convert.

I can't help but laugh at the idea of the civics test they give you when you apply for citizenship: As someone who has published law review articles on American constitutional law, I'm fairly certain I know more about civics than the vast majority of native-born American citizens. Not for nothing, I also speak fluent Mandarin, which I hear is a valuable skill these days. Nevertheless, soon I won't be able to use these skills to help the US economy—America is turning me away, requiring me to find work elsewhere.

The immigration system also undermines the US economy in smaller, more subtle ways. For example, during my first year at a law firm, a senior partner wanted me to travel with him to China on business. I had to explain to him that I could not do so because Homeland Security was still processing my visa application, and had I traveled abroad at that juncture I might not have been allowed back. Needless to say, the episode did not help my career or the firm's business.

I've already talked about my friends who think becoming a citizen is as easy as going to a government office and signing some papers. But even people whose job it is to understand the system often don't see how broken it is. At one firm where I worked, an HR manager told me to "just get married." Marriage solely for the sake of a green card is, of course, illegal—it is fraud upon the federal government. A bona fide marriage is fine, but that depends on you finding the right person and having your relationship progress according to Homeland Security's timeline. Once again there is the humiliating feeling that your life is not your own: the government may now effectively dictate when you get married.

25   In addition, a popular position for politicians posturing on television is to say that they favor immigration, just not illegal immigration, or that undocumented immigrants ought to get to the back of the line, otherwise the system would be unfair to legal immigrants. Guess

what? The system is already unfair to legal immigrants. And if the political class actually favored legal immigration, it certainly could have done any number of things to fix the problems I have described. If the political class actually favored legal immigration, I should not have to pack my bags right now.

So I'll be off. I'll travel for a while and then see where I end up, somewhere on this earth that is not America. I don't know what I'll do yet, but who knows, maybe I'll start a company and create some (non-American) jobs. And I am not alone: surveys show that of students from abroad studying at certain US universities, only 6 percent from India, 10 percent from China, and 15 percent from Europe expect to stay in America permanently, in large part because of the difficulties of the American immigration system.

In short, American immigration law hangs a Damocles's sword over the heads of even the supremely talented among us, turning those heads prematurely white. Never mind the tired, the poor, or the huddled masses. When the rest of the world sends America its best and brightest, America says, "Go away."

The Separate Street-Car Law in New Orleans

A. R. Holcombe

After the Civil War and the failure of Reconstruction, "Jim Crow" laws began to proliferate, ostensibly to keep African-Americans "separate but equal" to whites. This article, by A. R. Holcombe, points out the injustice inherent in this concept. "The Separate Street-Car Law in New Orleans" was first published in Outlook *on November 29, 1902.*

On November 3 the "Jim Crow," or separate street-car, law went into effect in New Orleans. This law was passed at the last session of the Louisiana Legislature. By its terms the street railway companies are compelled to use separate cars for the carrying of white and colored passengers, or to fit the cars with wire screens or wooden partitions.

When the bill was introduced by Mr. Wilson, of Tangipahoa Parish—a parish, by the way, that hasn't a street-car in it—there followed a perfect hail-storm of editorials and letters to the press, some condemning or approving such a law i*n toto*, others discussing certain phases of or deductions from the law and its operation. One of the most surprising things about the discussion was the fact that popular opinion, so far as both races were concerned, was about equally divided on the matter. So strong, indeed, was the opposition that at one time the bill came near not passing, and had it not been for the fact that in Louisiana the negro is practically without political influence, it is almost certain that it would not have passed. In support of the measure there was, however, a strong following. It is neither unjust nor inaccurate to say that this following was made up principally of those who dislike the negro because he is the negro. This fact is indicated in the chief argument advanced by those supporting the measure, i.e., that refined women and men were forced to sit by and rub elbows with negroes.

Those who opposed the passage of the bill were led by one of the oldest, most conservative and representative daily newspapers in the South. They declared that such a law was neither necessary nor expedient. It is a well-known fact that negroes getting on street-cars choose to sit by negroes rather than by white people, and particularly is this so in the case of the badly dressed or otherwise objectionable kind. There are, to be sure, negroes who, pushing themselves forward, choose to sit by the best, the cleanest, and the most refined people in the car, but these negroes, as a rule, are themselves clean, well dressed, and, in some cases, refined. On the whole, therefore, it was thought to be very unusual that a negro would prefer to sit by a white person, and more so that a white person would be compelled to sit by a negro who, on account of his dress or uncleanliness, was obnoxious. Under the circumstances, the passage of the law was thought to be clearly unnecessary. And, being unnecessary, it was inexpedient, since, without subserving any good purpose, it would certainly provoke ill feeling and possibly friction between the races, as used to happen when the famous "star cars" of the fifties and sixties were operated.

To understand the different opinions expressed regarding the law by several groups of negroes in New Orleans, it is necessary to say a word about the negroes themselves. One group, that which is conducting the educational campaign recently described in The Outlook, favored the passage of the bill, but took no active part in the discussions. With a view to bringing about a friendlier feeling between the races, it is probably that these negroes would have advocated openly the separate car system had not a large number of their own race been strongly opposed to the measure. It was fear of alienating these, and of destroying the growing influence for good already existing, that this group of negroes kept silent. With hardly an exception, they kept away from the meetings and refused to discuss the question except privately or by anonymous communications to the press.

5   Another group of intelligent negroes, the class that take the leading part in the various non-religious organizations, openly opposed the bill, and took steps, after it was passed, to prevent the law affecting the negro population. An association of women attached to the Masonic Order proposed to run 'bus lines to accommodate negro passengers, and issued a call to the fifty or more negro organizations in New Orleans to send representatives to a meeting at which the question would be considered. Unfeasible as the scheme was, it nevertheless appealed strongly to the negroes, and at the meetings representatives from nearly all the organizations were present.

It was apparent from the discussions that the "ruling passion" back of it all was the sense of deep humiliation that negroes as a race should be considered unworthy to ride in conveyances with white people. The railway companies had announced their intention of putting wire screens in every car, and to have negroes occupy the rear seats. This idea of sitting behind screens, as if they were wild or obnoxious animals, was another fact contributing to their mortification. Many of them, it was said, took pride in keeping clean, in wearing good clothes, and in behaving well, as much because they could feel at ease in decent company as because it gave them other persona satisfaction. To exclude such negroes from compartments occupied by white people would, they said, be as unjust as it would be to force them to sit in compartments with unworthy representatives of their own race, whom they, as much as the white people, despised. It would be equally unjust to admit obnoxious white people to white compartments and exclude respectable negroes from enjoying the same privilege.

Probably the next most pronounced sentiment of the meetings was a demand for negroes to support one another in business enterprises. To the negroes, the strongest argument in favor of a 'bus line was the fact that it would be a negro enterprise supported by negro capital and conducted for the general benefit of the race in New Orleans. Out of this assertion grew many an urgent appeal for negroes to acquire property and contribute to the general welfare of other negroes by patronizing them in their businesses. This sentiment is growing stronger and stronger every day, and the results of it are more and more apparent. Negroes no longer wish to send their children to white teachers; negro patients demand the services of negro physicians; drugstores, saloons, grocery-stores, coal and wood shops—in fact, almost every retail business in the city—are conducted on a small scale by negroes, and patronized almost exclusively by members of that race.

Of course the plan to establish a 'bus line failed. Opposition to it grew as its impracticable features became known, and at the third or fourth meeting nothing more was heard of the idea. The prevailing statement then was that the meeting was for the purpose of devising means to better the negro's condition in New Orleans.

The most sensible suggestion came from a band of ten or twelve negroes, who met several times to oppose the 'bus line movement. This suggestion was that eligible negroes register and vote, and that ineligible ones become educated or acquire property in order to be able to exercise the franchise rights granted under the constitution of Louisiana. At the pro-'bus line meetings no such suggestion was hinted at, and even when it was suggested to the negro community by this small band of clear-headed men, it created absolutely no comment.

Some time before the law went into effect it had ceased to be   10 generally discussed by both negroes and whites. At no time during any of the discussions was there the least violence either in language or conduct, and throughout it all the negroes have retained the sympathy of a large part of the white population. There was, of course, no trouble in enforcing the law. What effect it has had on the number of negroes carried by the cars cannot be accurately known, but the conductors say that there has been a large falling off. Several prominent negroes have refused to be seen on a "Jim Crow" car. They prefer to walk. Others ride on the cars, but stand on the platforms rather than be forced to sit behind the screens.

But, whatever has been the bad or questionable effects of the law, there has been at least one good effect. It has been demonstrated that the negro has more friends among the intelligent white people of New Orleans than he has ever had before; that he is to-day regarded as more capable than ever before of those finer sentiments of which the white race is so justly proud.

Buck v. Bell

Oliver Wendell Holmes

Oliver Wendell Holmes (1841–1935) delivered this Supreme Court decision in 1927. It confirmed the right of states to sterilizepeople found to be "unfit," including the mentally and physically disabled. Though the decision is seen as an endorsement of the controversial practice of eugenics—improving the gene pool by eliminating sources of "defective" genes—it has never been overturned by the Supreme Court.

Mr. Justice Holmes delivered the opinion of the Court.

This is a writ of error to review a judgment of the Supreme Court of Appeals of the State of Virginia affirming a judgment of the Circuit Court of Amherst County by which the defendant in error, the superintendent of the State Colony for Epileptics and Feeble Minded, was ordered to perform the operation of salpingectomy upon Carrie Buck, the plaintiff in error, for the purpose of making her sterile. 143 Va. 310. The case comes here upon the contention that the statute authorizing the judgment is void under the Fourteenth Amendment as denying to the plaintiff in error due process of law and the equal protection of the laws.

Carrie Buck is a feeble minded white woman who was committed to the State Colony above mentioned in due form. She is the daughter of a feeble minded mother in the same institution, and the mother of an illegitimate feeble minded child. She was eighteen years old at the time of the trial of her case in the Circuit Court, in the latter part of 1924. An Act of Virginia, approved March 20, 1924, recites that the health of the patient and the welfare of society may be promoted in certain cases by the sterilization of mental defectives, under careful safeguard, &c.; that the sterilization may be effected in males by vasectomy and in females by salpingectomy, without serious pain or substantial danger to life; that the Commonwealth is supporting in various institutions many defective persons who, if now discharged, would become a menace, but, if incapable of procreating, might be discharged with safety and become self-supporting with benefit to themselves and to society, and that experience has shown that heredity plays an important part in the transmission of insanity, imbecility, &c. The statute then enacts that, whenever the superintendent of certain institutions, including the above-named State Colony, shall be of opinion that it is for the best interests of the patients and of society that an inmate under his care should be sexually sterilized, he may have the operation performed upon any patient afflicted with hereditary forms of insanity, imbecility, &c., on complying with the very careful provisions by which the act protects the patients from possible abuse.

The superintendent first presents a petition to the special board of directors of his hospital or colony, stating the facts and the grounds for his opinion, verified by affidavit. Notice of the petition and of the time and place of the hearing in the institution is to be served upon the inmate, and also upon his guardian, and if there is no guardian, the superintendent is to apply to the Circuit Court of the County to appoint one. If the inmate is a minor, notice also is to be given to his parents, if any, with a copy of the petition. The board is to see to it that the inmate may attend the hearings if desired by him or his guardian. The evidence is all to be reduced to writing, and, after the board has made its order for or against the operation, the superintendent, or the inmate, or his guardian, may appeal to the Circuit Court of the County. The Circuit Court may consider the record of the board and the evidence before it and such other admissible evidence as may be offered, and may affirm, revise, or reverse the order of the board and enter such order as it deems just. Finally any party may apply to the Supreme Court of Appeals, which, if it grants the appeal, is to hear the case upon the record of the trial in the Circuit Court, and may enter such order as it thinks the Circuit Court should have entered. There can be no doubt that, so far as procedure is concerned, the rights of the patient are most carefully considered, and, as every step in this case was taken in scrupulous compliance with the statute and after months of observation, there is no doubt that, in that respect, the plaintiff in error has had due process of law.

The attack is not upon the procedure, but upon the substantive 5 law. It seems to be contended that in no circumstances could such an order be justified. It certainly is contended that the order cannot be justified upon the existing grounds. The judgment finds the facts that have been recited, and that Carrie Buck "is the probable potential parent of socially inadequate offspring, likewise afflicted, that she may be sexually sterilized without detriment to her general health, and that her welfare and that of society will be promoted by her sterilization," and thereupon makes the order. In view of the general declarations of the legislature and the specific findings of the Court, obviously we cannot say as matter of law that the grounds do not exist, and, if they exist, they justify the result. We have seen more than once that the public welfare may call upon the best citizens for their lives. It would be strange if it could not call upon those who already sap the strength of the State for these lesser sacrifices, often not felt to be such by those concerned, in order to prevent our being swamped with incompetence. It is better for all the world if, instead of waiting to execute degenerate offspring for crime or to let them starve for their imbecility, society can prevent those who are manifestly unfit from continuing their kind. The principle that sustains compulsory vaccination is broad enough to cover cutting the Fallopian tubes (Jacobson v. Massachusetts, 197 U.S. 11). Three generations of imbeciles are enough.

But, it is said, however it might be if this reasoning were applied generally, it fails when it is confined to the small number who are in the institutions named and is not applied to the multitudes outside. It is the usual last resort of constitutional arguments to point out shortcomings of this sort. But the answer is that the law does all that is needed when it does all that it can, indicates a policy, applies it to all within the lines, and seeks to bring within the lines all similarly situated so far and so fast as its means allow. Of course, so far as the operations enable those who otherwise must be kept confined to be returned to the world, and thus open the asylum to others, the equality aimed at will be more nearly reached.

Judgment affirmed.

Mr. Justice Butler dissents.

Legends from Camp

Prologue

Lawson Fusao Inada

Lawson Fusao Inada was born in Fresno, California, in 1938 to second-generation Japanese immigrant parents. When he was four years old, he and his family were interned by the US government, along with other American citizens of Japanese descent, for the duration of World War II. Inada is a jazz musician and poet. He moved to Oregon in 1966 and, 40 years later, was appointed state Poet Laureate. This excerpt is from his book Legends from Camp, *which won the American Book Award in 1994.*

It began as truth, as fact.
That is, at least the numbers, the statistics,
are there for verification:

10 camps, 7 states,
120,113 residents.

Still, figures can lie: people are born, die.
And as for the names of the places themselves,
these, too, were subject to change:

Denson or Jerome, Arkansas;
Gila or Canal, Arizona;
Tule Lake or Newell, California;
Amache or Granada, Colorado.

As was the War Relocation Authority
with its mention of "camps" or "centers" for:

Assembly,
Concentration,
Detention,
Evacuation,
Internment,
Relocation, —
among others.

"Among others" — that's important also. Therefore, let's not forget
contractors, carpenters, plumbers, electricians and architects,
sewage engineers, and all the untold thousands who provided
the materials, decisions, energy, and transportation to make the
camps a success, including, of course, the administrators, clerks,
and families who not only swelled the population but were there
to make and keep things shipshape according to D.C. directives
and people deploying coffee in the various offices of the WRA,
overlooking, overseeing rivers, cityscapes, bays, whereas in actual
camp the troops — excluding, of course, our aunts and uncles
and sisters and brothers and fathers and mothers serving stateside,
in the South Pacific, the European theater — pretty much had
things in order; finally, there were the grandparents, who since
the turn of the century, simply assumed they were living in
America "among others."

The situation, obviously, was rather confusing.
It obviously confused simple people
who had simply assumed they were friends, neighbors,
colleagues, partners, patients, customers, students,

teachers, of, not so much "aliens" or "non-aliens,"
but likewise simple, unassuming people
who paid taxes as fellow citizens and populated
pews and desks and fields and places
of ordinary American society and commerce.

Rumors flew. Landed. What's what? Who's next?

And then, "just like that," it happened.
And then, "just like that," it was over.
Sun, moon, stars—they came, and went.

And then, and then, things happened,
and as they ended they kept happening,
and as they happened they ended
and began again, happening, happening,

until the event, the experience, the history,
slowly began to lose its memory,
gradually drifting into a kind of fiction—

a "true story based on fact,"
but nevertheless with "all the elements of fiction"—
and then, and then, sun, moon, stars,
we come, we come, to where we are:
Legend.

Instructions to All Persons of Japanese Ancestry

During World War II, more than 120,000 people living in the United States who had Japanese ancestry were incarcerated in what came to be known as internment camps. Over half of those imprisoned were United States citizens. This text is the notice — printed on large posters — to the San Francisco Bay Area that Japanese-Americans were to turn themselves in to military personnel for this internment. It was prepared by the Western Defense Command and Fourth Army Wartime Civil Control Administration.

Presidio of San Francisco, California
May 3, 1942
Instructions to All Persons of Japanese Ancestry Living in the Following Area:

All of that portion of the County of Alameda, State of California, within the boundary beginning at the point where the southerly limits of the City of Oakland meet San Francisco Bay; thence easterly and following the southerly limits of said city to U.S. Highway No. 50; thence southerly and easterly on said Highway No. 50 to its intersection with California State Highway No. 21; thence southerly on said Highway No. 21 to its intersection, at or near Warm Springs, with California State Highway No. 17; thence southerly on said Highway No. 17 to the Alameda-Santa Clara County line; thence westerly and following said county line to San Francisco Bay; thence northerly, and following the shoreline of San Francisco Bay to the point of Beginning.

5   Pursuant to the provisions of Civilian Exclusion Order No. 34, this Headquarters, dated May 3, 1942, all persons of Japanese ancestry, both alien and non-alien, will be evacuated from the above area by

12 o'clock noon, P. W. T., Sunday, May 9, 1942.

No Japanese person living in the above area will be permitted to change residence after 12 o'clock noon, P. W. T., Sunday, May 3, 1942, without obtaining special permission from the representative of the Commanding General, Northern California Sector, at the Civil Control Station located at:

920 "C" Street, Hayward, California.

Such permits will only be granted for the purpose of uniting members of a family, or in cases of grave emergency.

The Civil Control Station is equipped to assist the Japanese population affected by this evacuation in the following ways:

1. Give advice and instructions on the evacuation.

2. Provide services with respect to the management, leasing, sale, storage or other disposition of most kinds of property, such as real estate, business and professional equipment, household goods, boats, automobiles and livestock.

3. Provide temporary residence elsewhere for all Japanese in family groups.

4. Transport persons and a limited amount of clothing and equipment to their new residence.

The Following Instructions Must Be Observed: 10

1. A responsible member of each family, preferably the head of the family, or the person in whose name most of the property is held, and each individual living alone, will report to the Civil Control Station to receive further instructions. This must be done between 8:00 A. M. and 5:00 P. M. on Monday, May 4, 1942, or between 9:00 A. M. and 5:00 P. M. on Tuesday, May 5, 1942.

2. Evacuees must carry with them on departure for the Assembly Center, the following property:

   a. Bedding and linens (no mattress) for each member of the family;

   b. Toilet articles for each member of the family;

   c. Extra clothing for each member of the family;

   d. Sufficient knives, forks, spoons, plates, bowls and cups for each member of the family;

   e. Essential personal effects for each member of the family.

All items carried will be securely packaged, tied and plainly marked with the name of the owner and numbered in accordance with instructions obtained at the Civil Control Station. The size and number of packages is limited to that which can be carried by the individual or family group.

3. No pets of any kind will be permitted.

4. No personal items and no household goods will be shipped to the Assembly Center.

5. The United States Government through its agencies will provide for the storage, at the sole risk of the owner, of the more substantial household items, such as iceboxes, washing machines, pianos and other heavy furniture. Cooking utensils and other small items will be accepted for storage if crated, packed and plainly marked with the name and address of the owner. Only one name and address will be used by a given family.

6. Each family, and individual living alone, will be furnished transportation to the Assembly Center or will be authorized to travel by private automobile in a supervised group. All instructions pertaining to the movement will be obtained at the Civil Control Station.

Go to the Civil Control Station between the hours of 8:00 A. M. and 5:00 P. M., Monday, May 4, 1942, or between the hours of 8:00 A.M. and 5:00 P. M., Tuesday, May 5, 1942, to receive further instructions.

J. L. Dewitt
Lieutenant General, U.S. Army Commanding

Second Address to Congress

Andrew Jackson

Andrew Jackson (1767–1845) was the seventh president of the United States, from 1829 to 1837. He also served as a member of the US Senate and House of Representatives and as a general in the US Army. In 1830, Jackson signed the Indian Removal Act, which relocated—sometimes forcibly—most Native American tribes in the South, in order to make room for white settlers. In his second annual message to Congress, Jackson defends this decision.

December 6, 1830

It gives me pleasure to announce to Congress that the benevolent policy of the government, steadily pursued for nearly thirty years, in relation to the removal of the Indians beyond the white settlements is approaching to a happy consummation. Two important tribes have accepted the provision made for their removal . . . and it is believed that their example will induce the remaining tribes also to seek the same obvious advantages.

The consequences of a speedy removal will be important to the United States, to individual States, and to the Indians themselves. . . . It puts an end to all possible danger of collision between the authorities of the General and State governments on account of the Indians. It will place a dense and civilized population in large parts of country now occupied by a few savage hunters. By opening the whole territory between Tennessee on the north and Louisiana on the south to the settlement of the whites it will incalculably strengthen the southwestern frontier and render the adjacent States strong enough to repel future invasions without remote aid. It will relieve the whole State of Mississippi and the western part of Alabama of Indian occupancy, and enable those States to advance rapidly in population, wealth and power. It will separate the Indians from immediate contact with settlements of whites; free them from the power of the States; enable them to pursue happiness in their own way and under their own rude institutions; will retard the progress of decay, which is lessening their numbers, and perhaps cause them gradually . . . to cast off their savage habits and become an interesting, civilized, and Christian community. . . .

Toward the aborigines of the country no one can indulge a more friendly feeling than myself, or would go further in attempting to reclaim them from their wandering habits and make them a happy, prosperous people. . . .

Humanity has often wept over the fate of the aborigines of this country. . . . To follow to the tomb the last of his race and to tread on the graves of extinct nations excite melancholy reflections. But true philanthropy reconciles the mind to these vicissitudes as it does to the extinction of one generation to make room for another. In the monuments and fortresses of an unknown people, spread over the extensive regions of the West, we behold the memorials of a once powerful race, which was exterminated or has disappeared to make room for the existing savage tribes. . . . What good man would prefer a country covered with forests and ranged by a few thousand savages to our extensive Republic, studded with cities, towns, and prosperous farms . . . and filled with all the blessings of liberty, civilization, and religion? . . .

Doubtless it will be painful to leave the graves of their fathers; but what do they more than our ancestors did or than our children are now doing. To better their condition in an unknown land our forefathers left all that was dear in earthly objects. . . . Can it be cruel in this Government when, by events which it cannot control, the Indian is made discontented in his ancient home, to purchase his lands, to give him a new and extensive territory, to pay the expense of his removal, and support him a year in his new abode? How many thousands of our own people would gladly embrace the opportunity of removing to the West on such conditions!

Seven Years Concealed

Harriet Ann Jacobs

Harriet Ann Jacobs (1813–1897) was an African-American writer who was born into slavery in North Carolina. Unable to bear repeated sexual harassment by her master, Jacobs escaped in 1835, at one point living for seven years in a crawl space in her grandmother's attic. She eventually settled in the Washington, D.C. area and worked to support freed slaves. Her memoir, which is excerpted here, was first published in 1861 and titled Incidents in the Life of a Slave Girl.

I. Childhood

I was born a slave; but I never knew it till six years of happy childhood had passed away. My father was a carpenter, and considered so intelligent and skillful in his trade, that, when buildings out of the common line were to be erected, he was sent for from long distances, to be head workman. On condition of paying his mistress two hundred dollars a year, and supporting himself, he was allowed to work at his trade, and manage his own affairs. His strongest wish was to purchase his children; but, though he several times offered his hard earnings for that purpose, he never succeeded. In complexion my parents were a light shade of brownish yellow, and were termed mulattoes. They lived together in a comfortable home; and, though we were all slaves, I was so fondly shielded that I never dreamed I was a piece of merchandise, trusted to them for safe keeping, and liable to be demanded of them at any moment. I had one brother, William, who was two years younger than myself—a bright, affectionate child. I had also a great treasure in my maternal grandmother, who was a remarkable woman in many respects. She was the daughter of a planter in South Carolina, who, at his death, left her mother and his three children free, with money to go to St. Augustine, where they had relatives. It was during the Revolutionary War; and they were captured on their passage, carried back, and sold to different purchasers. Such was the story my grandmother used to tell me; but I do not remember all the particulars. She was a little girl when she was captured and sold to the keeper of a large hotel. I have often heard her tell how hard she fared during childhood. But as she grew older she evinced so much intelligence, and was so faithful, that her master and mistress could not help seeing it was for their interest to take care of such a valuable piece of property. She became an indispensable personage in the household, officiating in all capacities, from cook and wet nurse to seamstress. She was much praised for her cooking; and her nice crackers became so famous in the neighborhood that many people were desirous of obtaining them. In consequence of numerous requests of this kind, she asked permission of her mistress to bake crackers at night, after all the household work was done; and she obtained leave to do it, provided she would clothe herself and her children from the profits. Upon these terms, after working hard all day for her mistress, she began her midnight bakings, assisted by her two oldest children. The business proved profitable; and each year she laid by a little, which was saved for a fund to purchase her children. Her master died, and the property was divided among his heirs. The widow had her dower in the hotel, which she continued to keep open. My grandmother remained in her service as a slave; but her children were divided among her master's children. As she had five, Benjamin, the youngest one, was sold, in order that each heir might have an equal portion of dollars and cents. There was so little difference in our ages that he seemed more like my brother than my uncle. He was a bright, handsome lad, nearly white; for he inherited the complexion my grandmother had derived from Anglo-Saxon ancestors. Though only ten years old, seven hundred and twenty dollars were paid for him. His sale was a terrible blow to my grandmother; but she was naturally hopeful, and she went to work with renewed energy, trusting in time to be able to purchase some of her children. She had laid up three hundred dollars, which her mistress one day begged as a loan, promising to pay her soon. The reader probably knows that no promise or writing given to a slave is legally binding; for, according to Southern laws, a slave, being property, can hold no property. When my grandmother lent her hard earnings to her mistress, she trusted solely to her honor. The honor of a slaveholder to a slave!

To this good grandmother I was indebted for many comforts. My brother Willie and I often received portions of the crackers, cakes, and preserves, she made to sell; and after we ceased to be children we were indebted to her for many more important services.

Such were the unusually fortunate circumstances of my early childhood. When I was six years old, my mother died; and then, for the first time, I learned, by the talk around me, that I was a slave. My mother's mistress was the daughter of my grandmother's mistress. She was the foster sister of my mother; they were both nourished at my grandmother's breast. In fact, my mother had been weaned at three months old, that the babe of the mistress might obtain sufficient food. They played together as children; and, when they became women, my mother was a most faithful servant to her whiter foster sister. On her death-bed her mistress promised that her children should never suffer for any thing; and during her lifetime she kept her word. They all spoke kindly of my dead mother, who had been a slave merely in name, but in nature was noble and womanly. I grieved for her, and my young mind was troubled with the thought who would now take care of me and my little brother. I was told that my home was now to be with her mistress; and I found it a happy one. No toilsome or disagreeable duties were imposed upon me. My mistress was so kind to me that I was always glad to do her bidding, and proud to labor for her as much as my young years would permit. I would sit by her side for hours, sewing diligently, with a heart as free from care as that of any free-born white child. When she thought I was tired, she would send me out to run and jump; and away I bounded, to gather berries or flowers to decorate her room. Those were happy days — too happy to last. The slave child had no thought for the morrow; but there came that blight, which too surely waits on every human being born to be a chattel.

When I was nearly twelve years old, my kind mistress sickened and died. As I saw the cheek grow paler, and the eye more glassy, how earnestly I prayed in my heart that she might live! I loved her; for she had been almost like a mother to me. My prayers were not answered. She died, and they buried her in the little churchyard, where, day after day, my tears fell upon her grave.

5   I was sent to spend a week with my grandmother. I was now old enough to begin to think of the future; and again and again I asked myself what they would do with me. I felt sure I should never find another mistress so kind as the one who was gone. She had promised my dying mother that her children should never suffer for any thing; and when I remembered that, and recalled her many proofs of attachment to me, I could not help having some hopes that she had left me free. My friends were almost certain it would be so. They thought she would be sure to do it, on account of my mother's love and faithful service. But, alas! we all know that the memory of a faithful slave does not avail much to save her children from the auction block.

After a brief period of suspense, the will of my mistress was read, and we learned that she had bequeathed me to her sister's daughter, a child of five years old. So vanished our hopes. My mistress had taught me the precepts of God's Word: "Thou shalt love thy neighbor as thyself." "Whatsoever ye would that men should do unto you, do ye even so unto them." But I was her slave, and I suppose she did not recognize me as her neighbor. I would give much to blot out from my memory that one great wrong. As a child, I loved my mistress; and, looking back on the happy days I spent with her, I try to think with less bitterness of this act of injustice. While I was with her, she taught me to read and spell; and for this privilege, which so rarely falls to the lot of a slave, I bless her memory.

She possessed but few slaves; and at her death those were all distributed among her relatives. Five of them were my grandmother's children, and had shared the same milk that nourished her mother's children. Notwithstanding my grandmother's long and faithful service to her owners, not one of her children escaped the auction block. These God-breathing machines are no more, in the sight of their masters, than the cotton they plant, or the horses they tend.

IV. The Jealous Mistress

I would ten thousand times rather that my children should be the half-starved paupers of Ireland than to be the most pampered among the slaves of America. I would rather drudge out my life on a cotton plantation, till the grave opened to give me rest, than to live with an unprincipled master and a jealous mistress. The felon's home in a penitentiary is preferable. He may repent, and turn from the error of his ways, and so find peace; but it is not so with a favorite slave. She is not allowed to have any pride of character. It is deemed a crime in her to wish to be virtuous.

Mrs. Flint possessed the key to her husband's character before

I was born. She might have used this knowledge to counsel and to screen the young and the innocent among her slaves; but for them she had no sympathy. They were the objects of her constant suspicion and malevolence. She watched her husband with unceasing vigilance; but he was well practiced in means to evade it. What he could not find opportunity to say in words he manifested in signs. He invented more than were ever thought of in a deaf and dumb asylum. I let them pass, as if I did not understand what he meant; and many were the curses and threats bestowed on me for my stupidity. One day he caught me teaching myself to write. He frowned, as if he was not well pleased, but I suppose he came to the conclusion that such an accomplishment might help to advance his favorite scheme. Before long, notes were often slipped into my hand. I would return them, saying, "I can't read them, sir." "Can't you?" he replied; "then I must read them to you." He always finished the reading by asking, "Do you understand?" Sometimes he would complain of the heat of the tea room, and order his supper to be placed on a small table in the piazza. He would seat himself there with a well-satisfied smile, and tell me to stand by and brush away the flies. He would eat very slowly, pausing between the mouthfuls. These intervals were employed in describing the happiness I was so foolishly throwing away, and in threatening me with the penalty that finally awaited my stubborn disobedience. He boasted much of the forbearance he had exercised towards me, and reminded me that there was a limit to his patience. When I succeeded in avoiding opportunities for him to talk to me at home, I was ordered to come to his office, to do some errand. When there, I was obliged to stand and listen to such language as he saw fit to address to me. Sometimes I so openly expressed my contempt for him that he would become violently enraged, and I wondered why he did not strike me. Circumstanced as he was, he probably thought it was better policy to be forbearing. But the state of things grew worse and worse daily. In desperation I told him that I must and would apply to my grandmother for protection. He threatened me with death, and worse than death, if I made any complaint to her. Strange to say, I did not despair. I was naturally of a buoyant disposition, and always I had hope of somehow getting out of his clutches. Like many a poor, simple slave before me, I trusted that some threads of joy would yet be woven into my dark destiny.

I had entered my sixteenth year, and every day it became more   10
apparent that my presence was intolerable to Mrs. Flint. Angry words frequently passed between her and her husband. He had never punished me himself, and he would not allow anybody else to punish me. In that respect, she was never satisfied; but, in her angry moods, no terms were too vile for her to bestow upon me. Yet I, whom she detested so bitterly, had far more pity for her than he had, whose duty it was to make her life happy. I never wronged her, or wished to wrong her; and one word of kindness from her would have brought me to her feet.

After repeated quarrels between the doctor and his wife, he announced his intention to take his youngest daughter, then four years old, to sleep in his apartment. It was necessary that a servant should sleep in the same room, to be on hand if the child stirred. I was selected for that office, and informed for what purpose that arrangement had been made. By managing to keep within sight of people, as much as possible during the day time, I had hitherto succeeded in eluding my master, though a razor was often held to my throat to force me to change this line of policy. At night I slept by the side of my great aunt, where I felt safe. He was too prudent to come into her room. She was an old woman, and had been in the family many years. Moreover, as a married man, and a professional man, he deemed it necessary to save appearances in some degree. But he resolved to remove the obstacle in the way of his scheme; and he thought he had planned it so that he should evade suspicion. He was well aware how much I prized my refuge by the side of my old aunt, and he determined to dispossess me of it. The first night the doctor had the little child in his room alone. The next morning, I was ordered to take my station as nurse the following night. A kind Providence interposed in my favor. During the day Mrs. Flint heard of this new arrangement, and a storm followed. I rejoiced to hear it rage.

After a while my mistress sent for me to come to her room. Her first question was, "Did you know you were to sleep in the doctor's room?"

"Yes, ma'am."

"Who told you?"

15 "My master."

"Will you answer truly all the questions I ask?"

"Yes, ma'am."

"Tell me, then, as you hope to be forgiven, are you innocent of what I have accused you?"

"I am."

20 She handed me a Bible, and said, "Lay your hand on your heart, kiss this holy book, and swear before God that you tell me the truth."

I took the oath she required, and I did it with a clear conscience.

"You have taken God's holy word to testify your innocence," said she. "If you have deceived me, beware! Now take this stool, sit down, look me directly in the face, and tell me all that has passed between your master and you."

I did as she ordered. As I went on with my account her color changed frequently, she wept, and sometimes groaned. She spoke in tones so sad, that I was touched by her grief. The tears came to my eyes; but I was soon convinced that her emotions arose from anger and wounded pride. She felt that her marriage vows were desecrated, her dignity insulted, but she had no compassion for the poor victim of her husband's perfidy. She pitied herself as a martyr; but she was incapable of feeling for the condition of shame and misery in which her unfortunate, helpless slave was placed.

Yet perhaps she had some touch of feeling for me; for when the conference was ended, she spoke kindly, and promised to protect me. I should have been much comforted by this assurance if I could have had confidence in it; but my experiences in slavery had filled me with distrust. She was not a very refined woman, and had not much control over her passions. I was an object of her jealousy, and, consequently, of her hatred; and I knew I could not expect kindness or confidence from her under the circumstances in which I was placed. I could not blame her. Slave-holders' wives feel as other women would under similar circumstances. The fire of her temper kindled from small sparks, and now the flame became so intense that the doctor was obliged to give up his intended arrangement.

I knew I had ignited the torch, and I expected to suffer for it afterwards; but I felt too thankful to my mistress for the timely aid she rendered me to care much about that. She now took me to sleep in a room adjoining her own. There I was an object of her especial care, though not of her especial comfort, for she spent many a sleepless night to watch over me. Sometimes I woke up, and found her bending over me. At other times she whispered in my ear, as though it was her husband who was speaking to me, and listened to hear what I would answer. If she startled me, on such occasions, she would glide stealthily away; and the next morning she would tell me I had been talking in my sleep, and ask who I was talking to. At last, I began to be fearful for my life. It had been often threatened; and you can imagine, better than I can describe, what an unpleasant sensation it must produce to wake up in the dead of night and find a jealous woman bending over you. Terrible as this experience was, I had fears that it would give place to one more terrible.

My mistress grew weary of her vigils; they did not prove satisfactory. She changed her tactics. She now tried the trick of accusing my master of crime, in my presence, and gave my name as the author of the accusation. To my utter astonishment, he replied, "I don't believe it; but if she did acknowledge it, you tortured her into exposing me." Tortured into exposing him! Truly, Satan had no difficulty in distinguishing the color of his soul! I understood his object in making this false representation. It was to show me that I gained nothing by seeking the protection of my mistress; that the power was still all in his own hands. I pitied Mrs. Flint. She was a second wife, many years the junior of her husband; and the hoary-headed miscreant was enough to try the patience of a wiser and better woman. She was completely foiled, and knew not how to proceed. She would gladly have had me flogged for my supposed false oath; but, as I have already stated, the doctor never allowed anyone to whip me. The old sinner was politic. The application of the lash might have led to remarks that would have exposed him in the eyes of his children and grandchildren. How often did I rejoice that I lived in a town where all the inhabitants knew each other! If I had been on a remote plantation, or lost among the multitude of a crowded city, I should not be a living woman at this day.

The secrets of slavery are concealed like those of the Inquisition. My master was, to my knowledge, the father of eleven slaves. But did the mothers dare to tell who was the father of their children? Did the other slaves dare to allude to it, except in whispers among themselves? No, indeed! They knew too well the terrible consequences.

My grandmother could not avoid seeing things which excited her suspicions. She was uneasy about me, and tried various ways to buy me; but the never-changing answer was always repeated: "Linda does not belong to me. She is my daughter's property, and I have no legal right to sell her." The conscientious man! He was too scrupulous to sell me; but he had no scruples whatever about committing a much greater wrong against the helpless young girl placed under his guardianship, as his daughter's property. Sometimes my persecutor would ask me whether I would like to be sold. I told him I would rather be sold to any body than to lead such a life as I did. On such occasions he would assume the air of a very injured individual, and reproach me for my ingratitude. "Did I not take you into the house, and make you the companion of my own children?" he would say. "Have I ever treated you like a negro? I have never allowed you to be punished, not even to please your mistress. And this is the recompense I get, you ungrateful girl!" I answered that he had reasons of his own for screening me from punishment, and that the course he pursued made my mistress hate me and persecute me. If I wept, he would say, "Poor child! Don't cry! don't cry! I will make peace for you with your mistress. Only let me arrange matters in my own way. Poor, foolish girl! you don't know what is for your own good. I would cherish you. I would make a lady of you. Now go, and think of all I have promised you."

I did think of it.

Reader, I draw no imaginary pictures of southern homes. I am telling you the plain truth. Yet when victims make their escape from this wild beast of Slavery, northerners consent to act the part of bloodhounds, and hunt the poor fugitive back into his den, "full of dead men's bones, and all uncleanness." Nay, more, they are not only willing, but proud, to give their daughters in marriage to slaveholders. The poor girls have romantic notions of a sunny clime, and of the flowering vines that all the year round shade a happy home. To what disappointments are they destined! The young wife soon learns that the husband, in whose hands she has placed her happiness, pays no regard to his marriage vows. Children of every shade of complexion play with her own fair babies, and too well she knows that they are born unto him of his own household. Jealousy and hatred enter the flowery home, and it is ravaged of its loveliness.

Southern women often marry a man knowing that he is the father of many little slaves. They do not trouble themselves about it. They regard such children as property, as marketable as the pigs on the plantation; and it is seldom that they do not make them aware of this by passing them into the slave-trader's hands as soon as possible, and thus getting them out of their sight. I am glad to say there are some honorable exceptions.

I have myself known two southern wives who exhorted their husbands to free those slaves towards whom they stood in a "parental relation;" and their request was granted. These husbands blushed before the superior nobleness of their wives' natures. Though they had only counselled them to do that which it was their duty to do, it commanded their respect, and rendered their conduct more exemplary. Concealment was at an end, and confidence took the place of distrust.

Though this bad institution deadens the moral sense, even in white women, to a fearful extent, it is not altogether extinct. I have heard southern ladies say of Mr. Such a one, "He not only thinks it no disgrace to be the father of those little niggers, but he is not ashamed to call himself their master. I declare, such things ought not to be tolerated in any decent society!"

Jim Crow Laws

After the Civil War, beginning in the 1890s, so-called Jim Crow laws were codified in the United States to ensure segregation of blacks and whites. The inferior and underfunded "separate but equal" institutions these laws engendered—schools, buses, swimming pools, restaurants, hotels, and much more—didn't begin to disappear until the passage of the Civil Rights Act in 1964. The following is a sample of Jim Crow laws from various states.

Education

The schools for white children and the schools for negro children shall be conducted separately. *Florida*

Any person . . . who shall be guilty of printing, publishing or circulating printed, typewritten or written matter urging or presenting for public acceptance or general information, arguments or suggestions in favor of social equality or of intermarriage between whites and negroes, shall be guilty of a misdemeanor and subject to fine or not exceeding five hundred (500.00) dollars or imprisonment not exceeding six (6) months or both. *Mississippi*

Separate free schools shall be established for the education of children of African descent; and it shall be unlawful for any colored child to attend any white school, or any white child to attend a colored school. *Missouri*

Books shall not be interchangeable between the white and colored schools, but shall continue to be used by the race first using them. *North Carolina*

5   Any instructor who shall teach in any school, college or institution where members of the white and colored race are received and enrolled as pupils for instruction shall be deemed guilty of a misdemeanor, and upon conviction thereof, shall be fined in any sum not less than ten dollars ($10.00) nor more than fifty dollars ($50.00) for each offense. *Oklahoma*

Any white person of such county may use the county free library under the rules and regulations prescribed by the commissioners' court and may be entitled to all the privileges thereof. Said court shall make proper provision for the negroes of said county to be served through a separate branch or branches of the county free library, which shall be administered by [a] custodian of the negro race under the supervision of the county librarian. *Texas*

Facilities

Every employer of white or negro males shall provide for such white or negro males reasonably accessible and separate toilet facilities. *Alabama*

No person or corporation shall require any white female nurse to nurse in wards or rooms in hospitals, either public or private, in which negro men are placed. *Alabama*

There shall be separate buildings [for juvenile detention], not nearer than one fourth mile to each other, one for white boys and one for negro boys. White boys and negro boys shall not, in any manner, be associated together or worked together. *Florida*

10   The officer in charge shall not bury, or allow to be buried, any colored persons upon ground set apart or used for the burial of white persons. *Georgia*

The board of trustees shall . . . maintain a separate building . . . on separate ground for the admission, care, instruction, and support of all blind persons of the colored or black race. *Louisiana*

There shall be maintained by the governing authorities of every hospital maintained by the state for treatment of white and colored patients separate entrances for white and colored patients and visitors, and such entrances shall be used by the race only for which they are prepared. *Mississippi*

The warden shall see that the white convicts shall have separate apartments for both eating and sleeping from the negro convicts. *Mississippi*

The Corporation Commission is hereby vested with power and authority to require telephone companies . . . to maintain separate booths for white and colored patrons when there is a demand for such separate booths. That the Corporation Commission shall determine the necessity for said separate booths only upon complaint of the people in the town and vicinity to be served after due hearing as now provided by law in other complaints filed with the Corporation Commission. *Oklahoma*

Leisure

It shall be unlawful for a negro and white person to play together or in company with each other at any game of pool or billiards. *Alabama*

It shall be unlawful for any amateur white baseball team to play baseball on any vacant lot or baseball diamond within two blocks of a playground devoted to the Negro race, and it shall be unlawful for any amateur colored baseball team to play baseball in any vacant lot or baseball diamond within two blocks of any playground devoted to the white race. *Georgia*

It shall be unlawful for colored people to frequent any park owned or maintained by the city for the benefit, use and enjoyment of white persons . . . and unlawful for any white person to frequent any park owned or maintained by the city for the use and benefit of colored persons. *Georgia*

All persons licensed to conduct a restaurant, shall serve either white people exclusively or colored people exclusively and shall not sell to the two races within the same room or serve the two races anywhere under the same license. *Georgia*

No colored barber shall serve as a barber [to] white women or girls. *Georgia*

20   The [Conservation] Commission shall have the right to make segregation of the white and colored races as to the exercise of rights of fishing, boating and bathing. *Oklahoma*

No persons, firms, or corporations, who or which furnish meals to passengers at station restaurants or station eating houses, in times limited by common carriers of said passengers, shall furnish said meals to white and colored passengers in the same room, or at the same table, or at the same counter. *South Carolina*

Every person . . . operating . . . any public hall, theatre, opera house, motion picture show or any place of public entertainment or public assemblage which is attended by both white and colored persons, shall separate the white race and the colored race and shall set apart and designate . . . certain seats therein to be occupied by white persons and a portion thereof, or certain seats therein, to be occupied by colored persons. *Virginia*

Relationships

The marriage of a person of Caucasian blood with a Negro, Mongolian, Malay, or Hindu shall be null and void. *Arizona*

Any negro man and white woman, or any white man and negro woman, who are not married to each other, who shall habitually live in and occupy in the nighttime the same room shall each be punished by imprisonment not exceeding twelve (12) months, or by fine not exceeding five hundred ($500.00) dollars. *Florida*

Any person . . . who shall rent any part of any such building to a negro [25] person or a negro family when such building is already in whole or in part in occupancy by a white person or white family, or vice versa when the building is in occupancy by a negro person or negro family, shall be guilty of a misdemeanor and on conviction thereof shall be punished by a fine of not less than twenty-five ($25.00) nor more than one hundred ($100.00) dollars or be imprisoned not less than 10, or more than 60 days, or both such fine and imprisonment in the discretion of the court. *Louisiana*

Transportation

All passenger stations in this state operated by any motor transportation company shall have separate waiting rooms or space and separate ticket windows for the white and colored races. *Alabama*

All railroad companies and corporations, and all persons running or operating cars or coaches by steam on any railroad line or track in the State of Maryland, for the transportation of passengers, are hereby required to provide separate cars or coaches for the travel and transportation of the white and colored passengers. *Maryland*

The . . . Utilities Commission . . . is empowered and directed to require the establishment of separate waiting rooms at all stations for the white and colored races. *North Carolina*

The Five-Sensed World

Helen Keller

Helen Keller (1880–1968) was an author, activist, and lecturer. When she was 19 months old, she became gravely ill, and lost the ability to see and hear. Although she had "home signs" that she used with her family, it wasn't until her work with Anne Sullivan (popularized in The Miracle Worker*) that she was able to communicate with the rest of the world. Keller was the first deaf-blind person to earn a bachelor's degree, graduating from Radcliffe College. She spoke around the world, advocating for disabled rights, workers' rights, and other causes.*

The poets have taught us how full of wonders is the night; and the night of blindness has its wonders, too. The only lightless dark is the night of ignorance and insensibility. We differ, blind and seeing, one from another, not in our senses, but in the use we make of them, in the imagination and courage with which we seek wisdom beyond our senses.

It is more difficult to teach ignorance to think than to teach an intelligent blind man to see the grandeur of Niagara. I have walked with people whose eyes are full of light, but who see nothing in wood, sea, or sky, nothing in city streets, nothing in books. What a witless masquerade is this seeing! It were far better to sail forever in the night of blindness, with sense and feeling and mind, than to be thus content with the mere act of seeing. They have the sunset, the morning skies, the purple of distant hills, yet their souls voyage through this enchanted world with a barren stare.

The calamity of the blind is immense, irreparable. But it does not take away our share of the things that count — service, friendship, humour, imagination, wisdom. It is the secret inner will that controls one's fate. We are capable of willing to be good, of loving and being loved, of thinking to the end that we may be wiser. We possess these spirit-born forces equally with all God's children. Therefore we, too, see the lightnings and hear the thunders of Sinai. We, too, march through the wilderness and the solitary place that shall be glad for us, and as we pass, God maketh the desert to blossom like the rose. We, too, go in unto the Promised Land to possess the treasures of the spirit, the unseen permanence of life and nature.

The blind man of spirit faces the unknown and grapples with it, and what else does the world of seeing men do? He has imagination, sympathy, humanity, and these ineradicable existences compel him to share by a sort of proxy in a sense he has not. When he meets terms of colour, light, physiognomy, he guesses, divines, puzzles out their meaning by analogies drawn from the senses he has. I naturally tend to think, reason, draw inferences as if I had five senses instead of three. This tendency is beyond my control; it is involuntary, habitual, instinctive. I cannot compel my mind to say "I feel" instead of "I see" or "I hear." The word "feel" proves on examination to be no less a convention than "see" and "hear" when I seek for words accurately to describe the outward things that affect my three bodily senses. When a man loses a leg, his brain persists in impelling him to use what he has not and yet feels to be there. Can it be that the brain is so constituted that it will continue the activity which animates the sight and the hearing, after the eye and the ear have been destroyed?

5   It might seem that the five senses would work intelligently together only when resident in the same body. Yet when two or three are left unaided, they reach out for their complements in another body, and find that they yoke easily with the borrowed team. When my hand aches from overtouching, I find relief in the sight of another. When

my mind lags, wearied with the strain of forcing out thoughts about dark, musicless, colourless, detached substance, it recovers its elasticity as soon as I resort to the powers of another mind which commands light, harmony, colour. Now, if the five senses will not remain disassociated, the life of the deaf-blind cannot be severed from the life of the seeing, hearing race.

The deaf-blind person may be plunged and replunged like Schiller's diver into seas of the unknown. But, unlike the doomed hero, he returns triumphant, grasping the priceless truth that his mind is not crippled, not limited to the infirmity of his senses. The world of the eye and the ear becomes to him a subject of fateful interest. He seizes every word of sight and hearing because his sensations compel it. Light and colour, of which he has no tactual evidence, he studies fearlessly, believing that all humanly knowable truth is open to him. He is in a position similar to that of the astronomer who, firm, patient, watches a star night after night for many years and feels rewarded if he discovers a single fact about it. The man deaf-blind to ordinary outward things, and the man deaf-blind to the immeasurable universe, are both limited by time and space; but they have made a compact to wring service from their limitations.

The bulk of the world's knowledge is an imaginary construction. History is but a mode of imagining, of making us see civilizations that no longer appear upon the earth. Some of the most significant discoveries in modern science owe their origin to the imagination of men who had neither accurate knowledge nor exact instruments to demonstrate their beliefs. If astronomy had not kept always in advance of the telescope, no one would ever have thought a telescope worth making. What great invention has not existed in the inventor's mind long before he gave it tangible shape?

A more splendid example of imaginative knowledge is the unity with which philosophers start their study of the world. They can never perceive the world in its entire reality. Yet their imagination, with its magnificent allowance for error, its power of treating uncertainty as negligible, has pointed the way for empirical knowledge.

In their highest creative moments the great poet, the great musician cease to use the crude instruments of sight and hearing. They break away from their sense-moorings, rise on strong, compelling wings of spirit far above our misty hills and darkened valleys into the region of light, music, intellect.

10   What eye hath seen the glories of the New Jerusalem? What ear hath heard the music of the spheres, the steps of time, the strokes of chance, the blows of death? Men have not heard with their physical sense the tumult of sweet voices above the hills of Judea nor seen the heavenly vision; but millions have listened to that spiritual message through many ages.

Our blindness changes not a whit the course of inner realities. Of us it is as true as it is of the seeing that the most beautiful world is always entered through the imagination. If you wish to be something that you are not,—something fine, noble, good,—you shut your eyes, and for one dreamy moment you are that which you long to be.

On the Removal
of Confederate Monuments

Mitch Landrieu

Mitchell Joseph Landrieu was elected mayor of New Orleans in 2010. New Orleans has a rich cultural history, which Landrieu evokes in this speech from May 2017, saying "This is the history we should never forget and one that we should never again put on a pedestal to be revered."

The soul of our beloved City is deeply rooted in a history that has evolved over thousands of years; rooted in a diverse people who have been here together every step of the way—for both good and for ill. It is a history that holds in its heart the stories of Native Americans—the Choctaw, Houma Nation, the Chitimacha. Of Hernando De Soto, Robert Cavelier, Sieur de La Salle, the Acadians, the Islenos, the enslaved people from Senegambia, Free People of Colorix, the Haitians, the Germans, both the empires of France and Spain. The Italians, the Irish, the Cubans, the south and central Americans, the Vietnamese and so many more.

You see—New Orleans is truly a city of many nations, a melting pot, a bubbling caldron of many cultures. There is no other place quite like it in the world that so eloquently exemplifies the uniquely American motto: e pluribus unum—out of many we are one. But there are also other truths about our city that we must confront. New Orleans was America's largest slave market: a port where hundreds of thousands of souls were bought, sold and shipped up the Mississippi River to lives of forced labor of misery of rape, of torture. America was the place where nearly 4,000 of our fellow citizens were lynched, 540 alone in Louisiana; where the courts enshrined 'separate but equal'; where Freedom riders coming to New Orleans were beaten to a bloody pulp. So when people say to me that the monuments in question are history, well what I just described is real history as well, and it is the searing truth.

And it immediately begs the questions, why there are no slave ship monuments, no prominent markers on public land to remember the lynchings or the slave blocks; nothing to remember this long chapter of our lives; the pain, the sacrifice, the shame . . . all of it happening on the soil of New Orleans. So for those self-appointed defenders of history and the monuments, they are eerily silent on what amounts to this historical malfeasance, a lie by omission. There is a difference between remembrance of history and reverence of it.

For America and New Orleans, it has been a long, winding road, marked by great tragedy and great triumph. But we cannot be afraid of our truth. As President George W. Bush said at the dedication ceremony for the National Museum of African American History & Culture, "A great nation does not hide its history. It faces its flaws and corrects them." So today I want to speak about why we chose to remove these four monuments to the Lost Cause of the Confederacy, but also how and why this process can move us towards healing and understanding of each other. So, let's start with the facts.

5   The historic record is clear, the Robert E. Lee, Jefferson Davis, and P.G.T. Beauregard statues were not erected just to honor these men, but as part of the movement which became known as The Cult of the Lost Cause. This 'cult' had one goal — through monuments and through other means — to rewrite history to hide the truth, which is that the Confederacy was on the wrong side of humanity. First erected over 166 years after the founding of our city and 19 years after the end of the Civil War, the monuments that we took down were

meant to rebrand the history of our city and the ideals of a defeated Confederacy. It is self-evident that these men did not fight for the United States of America, they fought against it. They may have been warriors, but in this cause they were not patriots. These statues are not just stone and metal. They are not just innocent remembrances of a benign history. These monuments purposefully celebrate a fictional, sanitized Confederacy; ignoring the death, ignoring the enslavement, and the terror that it actually stood for.

After the Civil War, these statues were a part of that terrorism as much as a burning cross on someone's lawn; they were erected purposefully to send a strong message to all who walked in their shadows about who was still in charge in this city. Should you have further doubt about the true goals of the Confederacy, in the very weeks before the war broke out, the Vice President of the Confederacy, Alexander Stephens, made it clear that the Confederate cause was about maintaining slavery and white supremacy. He said in his now famous 'cornerstone speech' that the Confederacy's "cornerstone rests upon the great truth, that the negro is not equal to the white man; that slavery—subordination to the superior race—is his natural and normal condition. This, our new government, is the first, in the history of the world, based upon this great physical, philosophical, and moral truth."

Now, with these shocking words still ringing in your ears . . . I want to try to gently peel from your hands the grip on a false narrative of our history that I think weakens us. And make straight a wrong turn we made many years ago—we can more closely connect with integrity to the founding principles of our nation and forge a clearer and straighter path toward a better city and a more perfect union.

Last year, President Barack Obama echoed these sentiments about the need to contextualize and remember all our history. He recalled a piece of stone, a slave auction block engraved with a marker commemorating a single moment in 1830 when Andrew Jackson and Henry Clay stood and spoke from it. President Obama said, "Consider what this artifact tells us about history . . . on a stone where day after day for years, men and women . . . bound and bought and sold and bid like cattle on a stone worn down by the tragedy of over a thousand bare feet. For a long time the only thing we considered important, the singular thing we once chose to commemorate as history with a plaque were the unmemorable speeches of two powerful men."

A piece of stone—one stone. Both stories were history. One story told. One story forgotten or maybe even purposefully ignored. As clear as it is for me today . . . for a long time, even though I grew up in one of New Orleans' most diverse neighborhoods, even with my family's long proud history of fighting for civil rights . . . I must have passed by those monuments a million times without giving them a second thought. So I am not judging anybody, I am not judging people. We all take our own journey on race.

10   I just hope people listen like I did when my dear friend Wynton Marsalis helped me see the truth. He asked me to think about all the people who have left New Orleans because of our exclusionary attitudes. Another friend asked me to consider these four monuments from the perspective of an African American mother or father trying to explain to their fifth grade daughter who Robert E. Lee is and why he stands atop of our beautiful city. Can you do it? Can you look into that young girl's eyes and convince her that Robert E. Lee is there to encourage her? Do you think she will feel inspired and hopeful by that story? Do these monuments help her see a future with limitless potential? Have you ever thought that if her potential is limited, yours and mine are too? We all know the answer to these very simple questions. When you look into this child's eyes is the moment when the searing truth comes into focus for us. This is the moment when we

know what is right and what we must do. We can't walk away from this truth.

And I knew that taking down the monuments was going to be tough, but you elected me to do the right thing, not the easy thing and this is what that looks like. So relocating these Confederate monuments is not about taking something away from someone else. This is not about politics, this is not about blame or retaliation. This is not a naïve quest to solve all our problems at once.

This is, however, about showing the whole world that we as a city and as a people are able to acknowledge, understand, reconcile and most importantly, choose a better future for ourselves making straight what has been crooked and making right what was wrong. Otherwise, we will continue to pay a price with discord, with division and yes with violence.

To literally put the Confederacy on a pedestal in our most prominent places of honor is an inaccurate recitation of our full past. It is an affront to our present, and it is a bad prescription for our future. History cannot be changed. It cannot be moved like a statue. What is done is done. The Civil War is over, and the Confederacy lost and we are better for it. Surely we are far enough removed from this dark time to acknowledge that the cause of the Confederacy was wrong.

And in the second decade of the 21st century, asking African Americans—or anyone else—to drive by property that they own; occupied by reverential statues of men who fought to destroy the country and deny that person's humanity seems perverse and absurd. Centuries old wounds are still raw because they never healed right in the first place. Here is the essential truth. We are better together than we are apart.

Indivisibility is our essence. Isn't this the gift that the people of New Orleans have given to the world? We radiate beauty and grace in

15

our food, in our music, in our architecture, in our joy of life, in our celebration of death; in everything that we do. We gave the world this funky thing called jazz, the most uniquely American art form that is developed across the ages from different cultures. Think about second lines, think about Mardi Gras, think about muffaletta, think about the Saints, gumbo, red beans and rice. By God, just think.

All we hold dear is created by throwing everything in the pot; creating, producing something better; everything a product of our historic diversity. We are proof that out of many we are one—and better for it! Out of many we are one—and we really do love it! And yet, we still seem to find so many excuses for not doing the right thing. Again, remember President Bush's words, "A great nation does not hide its history. It faces its flaws and corrects them."

We forget, we deny how much we really depend on each other, how much we need each other. We justify our silence and inaction by manufacturing noble causes that marinate in historical denial. We still find a way to say 'wait'/not so fast, but like Dr. Martin Luther King Jr. said, "wait has almost always meant never." We can't wait any longer. We need to change. And we need to change now.

No more waiting. This is not just about statues, this is about our attitudes and behavior as well. If we take these statues down and don't change to become a more open and inclusive society this would have all been in vain. While some have driven by these monuments every day and either revered their beauty or failed to see them at all, many of our neighbors and fellow Americans see them very clearly. Many are painfully aware of the long shadows their presence casts; not only literally but figuratively. And they clearly receive the message that the Confederacy and the cult of the lost cause intended to deliver.

Earlier this week, as the cult of the lost cause statue of P.G.T. Beauregard came down, world renowned musician Terence Blanchard stood watch, his wife Robin and their two beautiful daughters at their side. Terence went to a high school on the edge of City Park named after one of America's greatest heroes and patriots, John F. Kennedy. But to get there he had to pass by this monument to a man who fought to deny him his humanity.

He said, "I've never looked at them as a source of pride . . . it's always made me feel as if they were put there by people who don't respect us. This is something I never thought I'd see in my lifetime. It's a sign that the world is changing." Yes, Terence, it is and it is long overdue. Now is the time to send a new message to the next generation of New Orleanians who can follow in Terence and Robin's remarkable footsteps.

A message about the future, about the next 300 years and beyond; let us not miss this opportunity New Orleans and let us help the rest of the country do the same. Because now is the time for choosing. Now is the time to actually make this the City we always should have been, had we gotten it right in the first place.

We should stop for a moment and ask ourselves — at this point in our history — after Katrina, after Rita, after Ike, after Gustav, after the national recession, after the BP oil catastrophe and after the tornado — if presented with the opportunity to build monuments that told our story or to curate these particular spaces . . . would these monuments be what we want the world to see? Is this really our story?

We have not erased history; we are becoming part of the city's history by righting the wrong image these monuments represent and crafting a better, more complete future for all our children and for future generations. And unlike when these Confederate monuments were first erected as symbols of white supremacy, we now have a chance to create not only new symbols, but to do it together, as one people. In our blessed land we all come to the table of democracy as equals. We have to reaffirm our commitment to a future where each citizen is guaranteed the uniquely American gifts of life, liberty and the pursuit of happiness.

That is what really makes America great and today it is more important than ever to hold fast to these values and together say a self-evident truth that out of many we are one. That is why today we reclaim these spaces for the United States of America. Because we are one nation, not two; indivisible with liberty and justice for all . . . not some. We all are part of one nation, all pledging allegiance to one flag, the flag of the United States of America. And New Orleanians are in . . . all of the way. It is in this union and in this truth that real patriotism is rooted and flourishes. Instead of revering a 4-year brief historical aberration that was called the Confederacy we can celebrate all 300 years of our rich, diverse history as a place named New Orleans and set the tone for the next 300 years.

25   After decades of public debate, of anger, of anxiety, of anticipation, of humiliation and of frustration. After public hearings and approvals from three separate community led commissions. After two robust public hearings and a 6–1 vote by the duly elected New Orleans City Council. After review by 13 different federal and state judges. The full weight of the legislative, executive and judicial branches of government has been brought to bear and the monuments in accordance with the law have been removed. So now is the time to come together and heal and focus on our larger task. Not only building new symbols, but making this city a beautiful manifestation of what is possible and what we as a people can become.

Let us remember what the once exiled, imprisoned and now universally loved Nelson Mandela and what he said after the fall of apartheid. "If the pain has often been unbearable and the revelations shocking to all of us, it is because they indeed bring us the beginnings of a common understanding of what happened and a steady restoration of the nation's humanity." So before we part let us again state the truth clearly.

The Confederacy was on the wrong side of history and humanity. It sought to tear apart our nation and subjugate our fellow Americans to slavery. This is the history we should never forget and one that we should never again put on a pedestal to be revered. As a community, we must recognize the significance of removing New Orleans' Confederate monuments. It is our acknowledgment that now is the time to take stock of, and then move past, a painful part of our history.

Anything less would render generations of courageous struggle and soul-searching a truly lost cause. Anything less would fall short of the immortal words of our greatest President Abraham Lincoln, who with an open heart and clarity of purpose calls on us today to unite as one people when he said: "With malice toward none, with charity for all, with firmness in the right, as God gives us to see the right, let us strive on to finish the work we are in, to bind up the nation's wounds . . . to do all which may achieve and cherish—a just and lasting peace among ourselves and with all nations.

The New Colossus

Emma Lazarus

Emma Lazarus (1849–1887) was born into a large Jewish family in New York City, where she lived her whole life. A poet and writer, she is best known for her sonnet "The New Colossus," which she wrote in 1883 as a donation for an auction to raise funds to build a pedestal for the Statue of Liberty. Her poem was later engraved on a plaque at the base of the statue, which she calls "Mother of Exiles."

Not like the brazen giant of Greek fame,
With conquering limbs astride from land to land;
Here at our sea-washed, sunset gates shall stand
A mighty woman with a torch, whose flame
Is the imprisoned lightning, and her name
Mother of Exiles. From her beacon-hand
Glows world-wide welcome; her mild eyes command
The air-bridged harbor that twin cities frame.

"Keep, ancient lands, your storied pomp!" cries she
With silent lips. "Give me your tired, your poor,
Your huddled masses yearning to breathe free,
The wretched refuse of your teeming shore.
Send these, the homeless, tempest-tost to me,
I lift my lamp beside the golden door!"

My Husband Is a Cop

This essay was written by the wife of a law enforcement officer, who wishes to remain anonymous. It was first published in the July 2016 edition of Vox *(www.vox.com).*

Exactly 17 minutes after his change of shift is when I take my first deep breath of the day. My husband's car door slams shut, and he walks into the house.

I hear that shink of the metal-on-metal slide as his 9mm duty weapon gets unloaded and locked away. After the heavy thud-click of the safe door latching, I hear the rip of the 6-inch heavy-duty elasticized Velcro bands torn from either side of my husband's torso, and he has freed himself from the cage of lifesaving Kevlar.

He strips away the day along with the almost 50 pounds of gear, both safety and utility, that he wears around his waist and on his body as matter-of-factly as a salesman wears a suit and a nurse wears scrubs. The water runs and the hot water tank clunks as he washes the accumulated dirt of the day off himself.

Either he reheats the dinner plate we made for him hours ago, unappetizingly congealed in the fridge under plastic wrap, or he's just tired enough to come right to bed despite a 12-hour shift without a break long enough to eat.

I am a veteran police officer's wife with more than two decades of 5 marriage and almost the same amount of time with my husband on the job. These are the normal, comforting sounds of my night. Our kids are asleep, the house is quiet, and my husband is alive. It's a good night to be me.

Last Thursday night was not a good night to be the wife of Brent Thompson — the Dallas transit police officer who was shot to death by a sniper — or any of the four other Dallas police officers who also died in the shooting. Wednesday night was not a good night to be the girlfriend of Philando Castile. Tuesday night was not a good night to be the children of Alton Sterling.

Today I am not a widow, but so many others can't say the same.

We are liberals.

Our family, especially our cop, feel deeply and strongly advocate for changes in social policy that help people when they need it, and to educate others so they understand that this is for the benefit of our country.

10   We support smart people who have the courage to take positions of power and prominence, figure out a better way for our society to go forward, and fight to make this law. We view freedom as freedom from guns, freedom from debt due to illness or education, and freedom from schools that preach ignorance and conformity.

Our politics put us in a minority among my husband's fellow police officers and their families. We shake our heads at our misguided peers as they cling to the false security conservatism gives them and try not to become overtly hostile or involved in the circular logic that is cunningly fed to frightened people.

Our children don't mix with others from the department; we are not in the "in" crowd, we have sought our social outlets elsewhere, and we generally try not to agitate anyone with our "crazy ideas" about how the very politicians who prostrate themselves in paroxysmal patriotic "thank yous" are actively voting for legislation that guts our benefits and culls our numbers.

That's why I'm writing this piece anonymously and not identifying the suburb where we live – I don't want to get my husband in trouble at work, or to identify my children as targets.

According to my husband, if a politician says, "You guys are do-ing great!" and, "I am tough on crime!" they will carry 95 percent of the law enforcement community vote, even if it's a Republican who in the next breath wants to cut cops' pay, eliminate their retirement plan, and leave them to deal with 10-year-old squad cars and the firing of the 10 to 12 newest officers, all due to budget cuts.

This drives my husband crazy. He passionately advocates for de-criminalization, pardons, drug treatment plans, and generous public mental health treatment. He has hands-on experience with address-ing the unfortunate outcomes that stem from these social injustices and inequalities, and can't understand why anyone, including his co-workers, would not.

Our children are nearing adolescence and adulthood, and not one of them has held a firearm. We are gun owners, and even our adult children can't access the safe unless we both die; we have dis-posal instructions with our attorney that we drew up when they were all minors.

Our gun hygiene is impeccable, and I will dismiss a person from my mental radar as being fit to socialize with if they allow even a sin-gle stray bullet into the washing machine.

It's a cop wife trope—"ha ha, bullets in the washing ma-chine"—and it's a terrifying spiral into further ignorance and poten-tial harm. Unloading the magazine and removing the bullet from the chamber, putting a trigger lock on and locking the safe doesn't take more than 30 seconds.

None of our children has ever touched or held my husband's duty weapon. Why should they? In 21 years, he has only fired his weapon on the range.

If any of the children choose to become police officers, they can 20 learn to shoot at academy, or they can go to the range after they turn 18 with their father if they are curious. So far, neither of the kids who have already turned 18 has shown an iota of interest in a weapon, and I am secure in what I consider successful parenting.

They are all strong, smart, able to start a fire without a match, change a tire and the oil on their cars as applicable, throw a punch, make a splint, and catch and clean a fish; they have enough AP credits between the older two of the four to have earned a degree. Our family motto is taken from a Robert Heinlein quote: "Specialization is for insects."

We are fortunate to live in a large suburb with superior schools, houses maintained either professionally or by dedicated DIYers; our demographics skew toward mostly four-year college graduates with a significant percentage holding advanced degrees. Our police department is funded well enough for the officers to not only afford to live in town but to purchase their own homes here, and they are encouraged to do so. So we did.

However, a town that is able to pay patrol officers six-figure incomes demand the excellence that comes along with that expenditure. Our town puts forth an image of harmonious multiculturalism, and there is a zero-tolerance policy for any officer who displays racist or sexist behaviors either on or off the clock. Their ticketing and arrest statistics are analyzed constantly. They were early backseat, dashboard, and body camera adopters.

There are rigorous prescreening standards for the pool of officer hopefuls, and even after four out of a pool of a thousand applicants are accepted as trainees, the individual psychological, physical, and didactic training is intense. The continuing education is evidence-based and a yearly requirement.

25   The policymakers in the department and township are open to

change as the science evolves. This culminates in a culture where officers are taught to think flexibly, quickly, and fairly.

Due to the zero-tolerance policy in the department my husband works for, it's very rare for someone to make it past the initial psychological evaluation if they are even slightly biased in a way that could reflect poorly on the community.

This multiple-part test—oral, written, and small panel interview—is given over a course of a few weeks throughout the testing process. I'm sure it's even been refined in the 22 years since we went through the process.

It's draining, but so is standing on the witness stand having to explain your course of action to a grand jury, a judge, a lawyer, your boss, your spouse, parents, and children.

As in real life as well as "cop life," there is a huge disparity among police departments throughout the country. Small municipalities that pay their officers $12 an hour and require a GED provide their officers with minimal training in comparison to what I explained above, and their pool of applicants is limited by both pay and location. Anyone worthy of better has already left the area. These are not people who wish to understand the concept of meta-analysis and probably mock those who do.

Many people demand that the person who educates their child to 30 carry advanced degrees but do not wish to contribute to the additional training and continuing education for the person who may have to make a split second decision whether or not to kill their child.

I don't know about you, but I want someone who has studied and been screened and trained and reviewed and trained some more before even being allowed a weapon.

Liberals are correct about the fact that cops don't want to talk to them about the decision-making process that led them to act or not act in any given situation. They have the reason completely wrong. Officers don't want to speak for "all cops," because "all cops" are not hired, paid, or trained equally. They also may be prevented from doing so by departmental policy or legally depending on the situation.

Police officers have no choice but to go and confront what is presented, under chaotic conditions, expected to react in a split second and to do so each and every time in a way deemed perfect by someone examining it from the comfort of a chair with all the background information. That is why courts give cops the benefit of the doubt.

That is why they don't even bother explaining when the outrage occurs when a police officer is not charged with a crime, when all the information is gathered and it is perceived as "closing ranks" or a "good old boys' club."

35 An officer has to make a life-changing decision in a frighteningly short amount of time when the world is ending around everyone involved. This is why I relax when I hear the Velcro. This is why I have tried and failed to somehow defend the fact that my husband is not some sort of sociopathic monster.

Cops like my husband are exhausted by the amateur lawyers with 20/20 hindsight who feel they would do better at making a decision in an eighth of a second after they spent a few hours rewinding and replaying the video. Plenty of video is replayed and analyzed and picked apart frame by frame in a professional continuing education setting; the experienced 20/20 hindsight analysis by fellow professionals will be productive and contribute to the cognitive process that has to happen in a life-or-death situation.

They take this additional knowledge they gain from the input of their colleagues and superiors and trainers and continue to head in the direction of chaos and trouble, to save you or someone you love without checking to see if you have favorable opinions about the police.

On Friday morning, my husband sat on the edge of our bed and said, "Don't check your Twitter feed or your Facebook page yet. There was a sniper in Dallas that killed five police officers."

I didn't wake up a widow on Friday. I say this with a heavy heart and the weight of so many families, those of the Dallas five, the Sterling family, and the Castile family as well. To be human is to mourn life in such a terrible and senseless way. I blame the guns, not the cops. I look to my representatives in the federal government whom I trusted to keep people safe, and I ask them why. How many people need to die?

Squatter

Scott Nadelson

Scott Nadelson lives in Salem, Oregon, and teaches creative writing at Willamette University and Pacific Lutheran University. He is the author of a novel, a memoir, and three collections of short stories, one of which—Saving Stanley: The Brickman Stories, *about a Jewish family in suburban New Jersey*—*won the 2004 Oregon Book Award for fiction. "Squatter" ponders the existence of the person who briefly lived in Nadelson's vacant home.*

He broke in the day after we moved out, so he'd likely been watching the place for some time—maybe since the realtor first put a sign in the yard. That was three months earlier, but we'd yet to get an offer on the house. It was mid-2011, the market still sinking to undetermined depths, and even at thirty thousand less than what we'd paid for it, few people were interested in walking through. But this guy wanted to live here. He clearly appreciated the work we'd put into the old bungalow, remodeling kitchen and bathrooms, refinishing floors, replacing rotten boards on the deck. Afterward, from scattered evidence, we pieced together his visit. On the sliding glass door, two greasy smudges, the imprint of forehead and nose as he peered in to make sure no one had stayed behind. Then, around the side, footprints in the oxalis, where he tested one window after another until he discovered the one with the broken lock. What a thrill to feel the sash budge and then, crouching in the camellia, listen for the alarm that didn't sound. And how carefully he climbed in to avoid knocking over the lamp, to keep from soiling the armchair we'd left to stage the place for potential buyers. There were other things we'd left, too:

half a dozen dishes on the kitchen's open shelves, a few cast iron pans, air mattresses on cardboard boxes made up to look like beds. And in the garage a case of Riesling my father-in-law had given us when he thinned out his wine cellar, cast-offs we'd been storing for a year and never intended to drink. The stuff was sweet and warm, but our guy couldn't believe his luck when he found it, dragging the box inside, setting it in a place of prominence on the old farm table we used as a butcher block island in the middle of the kitchen floor. We hadn't left him a corkscrew—how thoughtless!—but he was resourceful enough to punch the cork in with a butter knife chisel and saucepan hammer. I don't know if it was before or after opening the first bottle that he decided to get some food. But eventually he let himself out the back door—which he left open a crack, maybe forgetfully, maybe for fresh air—and returned with a bag from Safeway. And what did he pick out? A tub of salad greens, bottles of oil and vinegar, scallions he sautéed in one of the cast iron pans, on the vintage Chambers stove we'd found on Craigslist. Salad! Sautéed scallions! Did he always eat this way? I want to believe it was a special night for him; that the house, though small and old and surrounded by decaying halfway houses and group homes for the mentally ill, was the most elegant he'd occupied for years; that he admired the people who lived here and had restored it so affectionately; that imagining them made him want to live as they did, cooking healthy food, drinking hand-me-down wine they couldn't afford to buy themselves. And what a night it was! The first bottle he finished while cooking, leaving it empty in the kitchen sink. The second he drank while eating his salad and a bag of tortilla chips on the air mattress in what had been our bedroom. Only he didn't realize it was an air mattress at first, because he sat on it hard, collapsing the cardboard boxes underneath. Salad dressing and wine spilled on the sheets, but he enjoyed his meal anyway, left

the plates on the mattress, and fetched a third bottle of Riesling. That
one he drank in the front bedroom, which had been my office, this
time taking the boxes away first and laying the air mattress on the
floor. Did he browse the dozen or so books I'd left on the shelf and
appreciate my taste in literature? Did he pass the time with a Chekhov
story—"The Kiss," maybe, or "The Darling"—or peruse recipes in
my vegetarian cookbook? All I know for sure is that here he spent the
night, getting up only once, as far as I could tell, to relieve himself on
the baseboard in the corner of the room. And why not? For tonight,
this was his house, and he could do with it what he pleased. If that
meant splattering urine on the wall and floor after downing three bottles of warm white wine, so be it. Why begrudge him that, when I'd
enjoyed so many nights here, strolling in the garden, cooking dinner
on the Chambers stove, making love under the cracked plaster ceilings, conceiving my daughter. How could I walk away from the place
just because it felt too small now that I had a child, the neighborhood
too dodgy, the school district's rating too low? Shouldn't I have done
more to honor all I'd put into it, all it had given me in return? I want
to believe my guy took in the perfect tight grain of the old floorboards
before laying down his head and shutting his eyes. I want to believe he
caught a glimpse of the moon made wavy by the leaded window, that
the surprise of it tickled out a little hiccup of laughter. I want to believe he slept a heavy sleep in my old office, that he dreamt swooning,
blissful dreams. Because I know it must have been a rough awakening
when the realtor opened the lockbox and jingled the key early the
next morning, leading in a young couple who wanted just this kind
of old place with a big yard, so long as it was free of rot, and its roof
didn't need replacing, and its sellers could come down another twenty
thousand off the asking price. How cruel to face the daylight slicing
through the tall windows; to scramble up from the floor and crouch

in the closet, waiting to run out the front door; to hear the couple ex-
claiming over high ceilings and laminate countertops they'd mistaken
for real marble; to hear the realtor shouting after him and telling the
couple to call the police; to feel the pavement rattling from shins to
throbbing head; to pass For Sale signs in the yards of sagging bun-
galows with patchwork siding and crumbling chimneys and weedy
lawns; and to know, once more, that nothing as ecstatic as love's first
flare ever lasts.

Howard University Commencement Address

Barack Obama

Barack Obama was the forty-fourth President of the United States. In 2016, he spoke at the commencement of Howard University, one of 107 HBCUs (Historically Black Colleges and Universities) in the United States. Most of the HBCUs were originally formed as a response to the vast majority of US colleges and universities that prohibited African-Americans from enrolling. Obama's speech at Howard encourages students to be grateful for the present, mindful of the past, and to keep working toward a better future.

To President Frederick, the Board of Trustees, faculty and staff, fellow recipients of honorary degrees, thank you for the honor of spending this day with you. And congratulations to the Class of 2016! (Applause.)

I know you're all excited today. You might be a little tired, as well. Some of you were up all night making sure your credits were in order. (Laughter.)

But you got here. And you've all worked hard to reach this day. You've shuttled between challenging classes and Greek life. You've led clubs, played an instrument or a sport. You volunteered, you interned. You held down one, two, maybe three jobs. You've made lifelong friends and discovered exactly what you're made of. The "Howard Hustle" has strengthened your sense of purpose and ambition.

Which means you're part of a long line of Howard graduates. Some are on this stage today. Some are in the audience. That spirit of achievement and special responsibility has defined this campus ever since the Freedman's Bureau established Howard just four years after the Emancipation Proclamation; just two years after the Civil War came to an end. They created this university with a vision — a vision of uplift; a vision for an America where our fates would be determined not by our race, gender, religion, or creed, but where we would be free — in every sense — to pursue our individual and collective dreams.

It is that spirit that's made Howard a centerpiece of African-American intellectual life and a central part of our larger American story. This institution has been the home of many firsts: the first black Nobel Peace Prize winner. The first black Supreme Court justice. But its mission has been to ensure those firsts were not the last. Countless scholars, professionals, artists, and leaders from every field received their training here. The generations of men and women who walked through this yard helped reform our government, cure disease, grow a black middle class, advance civil rights, shape our culture. The seeds of change — for all Americans — were sown here. And that's what I want to talk about today.

As I was preparing these remarks, I realized that when I was first elected President, most of you — the Class of 2016 — were just starting high school. Today, you're graduating college. I used to joke about being old. Now I realize I'm old. (Laughter.) It's not a joke anymore. (Laughter.)

But seeing all of you here gives me some perspective. It makes me reflect on the changes that I've seen over my own lifetime. So let me begin with what may sound like a controversial statement — a hot take.

Given the current state of our political rhetoric and debate, let me say something that may be controversial, and that is this: America is a better place today than it was when I graduated from college. (Applause.) Let me repeat: America is by almost every measure better than it was when I graduated from college. It also happens to be better off than when I took office — (laughter) — but that's a longer story. (Applause.) That's a different discussion for another speech.

But think about it. I graduated in 1983. New York City, America's largest city, where I lived at the time, had endured a decade marked by crime and deterioration and near bankruptcy. And many cities were in similar shape. Our nation had gone through years of economic stagnation, the stranglehold of foreign oil, a recession where unemployment nearly scraped 11 percent. The auto industry was getting its clock cleaned by foreign competition. And don't even get me started on the clothes and the hairstyles. I've tried to eliminate all photos of me from this period. I thought I looked good. (Laughter.) I was wrong.

10   Since that year — since the year I graduated — the poverty rate is down. Americans with college degrees, that rate is up. Crime rates are down. America's cities have undergone a renaissance. There are more women in the workforce. They're earning more money. We've cut teen pregnancy in half. We've slashed the African American dropout rate by almost 60 percent, and all of you have a computer in your pocket that gives you the world at the touch of a button. In 1983, I was part of fewer than 10 percent of African Americans who graduated with a bachelor's degree. Today, you're part of the more than 20 percent who will. And more than half of blacks say we're better off than our parents were at our age — and that our kids will be better off, too.

So America is better. And the world is better, too. A wall came down in Berlin. An Iron Curtain was torn asunder. The obscenity of apartheid came to an end. A young generation in Belfast and London have grown up without ever having to think about IRA bombings. In just the past 16 years, we've come from a world without marriage equality to one where it's a reality in nearly two dozen countries. Around the world, more people live in democracies. We've lifted more than 1 billion people from extreme poverty. We've cut the child mortality rate worldwide by more than half.

America is better. The world is better. And stay with me now—race relations are better since I graduated. That's the truth. No, my election did not create a post-racial society. I don't know who was propagating that notion. That was not mine. But the election itself—and the subsequent one—because the first one, folks might have made a mistake. (Laughter.) The second one, they knew what they were getting. The election itself was just one indicator of how attitudes had changed.

In my inaugural address, I remarked that just 60 years earlier, my father might not have been served in a D.C. restaurant—at least not certain of them. There were no black CEOs of Fortune 500 companies. Very few black judges. Shoot, as Larry Wilmore pointed out last week, a lot of folks didn't even think blacks had the tools to be a quarterback. Today, former Bull Michael Jordan isn't just the greatest basketball player of all time—he owns the team. (Laughter.) When I was graduating, the main black hero on TV was Mr. T. (Laughter.) Rap and hip hop were counterculture, underground. Now, Shonda Rhimes owns Thursday night, and Beyoncé runs the world. (Laughter.) We're no longer only entertainers, we're producers, studio executives. No longer small business owners—we're CEOs, we're mayors, representatives, Presidents of the United States. (Applause.)

I am not saying gaps do not persist. Obviously, they do. Racism persists. Inequality persists. Don't worry—I'm going to get to that. But I wanted to start, Class of 2016, by opening your eyes to the moment that you are in. If you had to choose one moment in history in which you could be born, and you didn't know ahead of time who you were going to be — what nationality, what gender, what race, whether you'd be rich or poor, gay or straight, what faith you'd be born into — you wouldn't choose 100 years ago. You wouldn't choose the fifties, or the sixties, or the seventies. You'd choose right now. If you had to choose a time to be, in the words of Lorraine Hansberry, "young, gifted, and black" in America, you would choose right now. (Applause.)

15   I tell you all this because it's important to note progress. Because to deny how far we've come would do a disservice to the cause of justice, to the legions of foot soldiers; to not only the incredibly accomplished individuals who have already been mentioned, but your mothers and your dads, and grandparents and great grandparents, who marched and toiled and suffered and overcame to make this day possible. I tell you this not to lull you into complacency, but to spur you into action — because there's still so much more work to do, so many more miles to travel. And America needs you to gladly, happily take up that work. You all have some work to do. So enjoy the party, because you're going to be busy. (Laughter.)

Yes, our economy has recovered from crisis stronger than almost any other in the world. But there are folks of all races who are still hurting — who still can't find work that pays enough to keep the lights on, who still can't save for retirement. We've still got a big racial gap in economic opportunity. The overall unemployment rate is five percent, but the black unemployment rate is almost nine. We've still got an achievement gap when black boys and girls graduate high school and college at lower rates than white boys and white girls. Harriet Tubman may be going on the twenty, but we've still got a gender gap when a black woman working full-time still earns just 66 percent of what a white man gets paid. (Applause.)

We've got a justice gap when too many black boys and girls pass through a pipeline from underfunded schools to overcrowded jails. This is one area where things have gotten worse. When I was in college, about half a million people in America were behind bars. Today, there are about 2.2 million. Black men are about six times likelier to be in prison right now than white men.

Around the world, we've still got challenges to solve that threaten everybody in the 21st century—old scourges like disease and conflict, but also new challenges, from terrorism and climate change.

So make no mistake, Class of 2016—you've got plenty of work to do. But as complicated and sometimes intractable as these challenges may seem, the truth is that your generation is better positioned than any before you to meet those challenges, to flip the script.

Now, how you do that, how you meet these challenges, how you 20
bring about change will ultimately be up to you. My generation, like all generations, is too confined by our own experience, too invested in our own biases, too stuck in our ways to provide much of the new thinking that will be required. But us old-heads have learned a few things that might be useful in your journey. So with the rest of my time, I'd like to offer some suggestions for how young leaders like you can fulfill your destiny and shape our collective future—bend it in the direction of justice and equality and freedom.

First of all—and this should not be a problem for this group—be confident in your heritage. (Applause.) Be confident in your blackness. One of the great changes that's occurred in our country since I was your age is the realization there's no one way to be black. Take it from somebody who's seen both sides of debate about whether I'm black enough. (Laughter.) In the past couple months, I've had lunch with the Queen of England and hosted Kendrick Lamar in the Oval Office. There's no straitjacket, there's no constraints, there's no litmus test for authenticity.

Look at Howard. One thing most folks don't know about Howard is how diverse it is. When you arrived here, some of you were like, oh, they've got black people in Iowa? (Laughter.) But it's true—this class comes from big cities and rural communities, and some of you crossed oceans to study here. You shatter stereotypes. Some of you come from a long line of Bison. Some of you are the first in your family to graduate from college. (Applause.) You all talk different, you all dress different. You're Lakers fans, Celtics fans, maybe even some hockey fans. (Laughter.)

And because of those who've come before you, you have models to follow. You can work for a company, or start your own. You can go into politics, or run an organization that holds politicians accountable. You can write a book that wins the National Book Award, or you can write the new run of "Black Panther." Or, like one of your alumni, Ta-Nehisi Coates, you can go ahead and just do both. You can create your own style, set your own standard of beauty, embrace your own sexuality. Think about an icon we just lost—Prince. He blew up categories. People didn't know what Prince was doing. (Laughter.) And folks loved him for it.

You need to have the same confidence. Or as my daughters tell me all the time, "You be you, Daddy." (Laughter.) Sometimes Sasha puts a variation on it—"You do you, Daddy." (Laughter.) And because you're a black person doing whatever it is that you're doing, that makes it a black thing. Feel confident.

25   Second, even as we each embrace our own beautiful, unique, and valid versions of our blackness, remember the tie that does bind us as African Americans—and that is our particular awareness of injustice and unfairness and struggle. That means we cannot sleepwalk through life. We cannot be ignorant of history. (Applause.) We can't

meet the world with a sense of entitlement. We can't walk by a home-less man without asking why a society as wealthy as ours allows that state of affairs to occur. We can't just lock up a low-level dealer with-out asking why this boy, barely out of childhood, felt he had no other options. We have cousins and uncles and brothers and sisters who we remember were just as smart and just as talented as we were, but somehow got ground down by structures that are unfair and unjust.

And that means we have to not only question the world as it is, and stand up for those African Americans who haven't been so lucky—because, yes, you've worked hard, but you've also been lucky. That's a pet peeve of mine: people who have been successful and don't realize they've been lucky. That God may have blessed them; it wasn't nothing you did. So don't have an attitude. But we must expand our moral imaginations to understand and empathize with all people who are struggling, not just black folks who are strug-gling—the refugee, the immigrant, the rural poor, the transgender person, and yes, the middle-aged white guy who you may think has all the advantages, but over the last several decades has seen his world upended by economic and cultural and technological change, and feels powerless to stop it. You got to get in his head, too.

Number three: you have to go through life with more than just passion for change; you need a strategy. I'll repeat that. I want you to have passion, but you have to have a strategy. Not just awareness, but action. Not just hashtags, but votes.

You see, change requires more than righteous anger. It requires a program, and it requires organizing. At the 1964 Democratic Con-vention, Fannie Lou Hamer—all five-feet-four-inches tall—gave a fiery speech on the national stage. But then she went back home to Mississippi and organized cotton pickers. And she didn't have the tools and technology where you can whip up a movement in minutes. She had to go door to door. And I'm so proud of the new guard of black civil rights leaders who understand this. It's thanks in large part to the activism of young people like many of you, from Black Twitter to Black Lives Matter, that America's eyes have been opened—white, black, Democrat, Republican—to the real problems, for example, in our criminal justice system.

But to bring about structural change, lasting change, awareness is not enough. It requires changes in law, changes in custom. If you care about mass incarceration, let me ask you: how are you pressuring members of Congress to pass the criminal justice reform bill now pending before them? (Applause.) If you care about better policing, do you know who your district attorney is? Do you know who your state's attorney general is? Do you know the difference? Do you know who appoints the police chief and who writes the police training manual? Find out who they are, what their responsibilities are. Mobilize the community, present them with a plan, work with them to bring about change, hold them accountable if they do not deliver. Passion is vital, but you've got to have a strategy.

30   And your plan better include voting—not just some of the time, but all the time. (Applause.) It is absolutely true that 50 years after the Voting Rights Act, there are still too many barriers in this country to vote. There are too many people trying to erect new barriers to voting. This is the only advanced democracy on Earth that goes out of its way to make it difficult for people to vote. And there's a reason for that. There's a legacy to that.

But let me say this: even if we dismantled every barrier to voting, that alone would not change the fact that America has some of the lowest voting rates in the free world. In 2014, only 36 percent of Americans turned out to vote in the midterms—the second-lowest participation rate on record. Youth turnout—that would be you—was less than 20 percent. Less than 20 percent. Four out of five did not vote. In 2012, nearly two in three African Americans turned out. And then, in 2014, only two in five turned out. You don't think that made a difference in terms of the Congress I've got to deal with? And then people are wondering, well, how come Obama hasn't gotten this done? How come he didn't get that done? You don't think that made a difference? What would have happened if you had turned out at 50, 60, 70 percent, all across this country? People try to make this political thing really complicated. Like, what kind of reforms do we need? And how do we need to do that? You know what, just vote. It's math. If you have more votes than the other guy, you get to do what you want. (Laughter.) It's not that complicated.

And you don't have excuses. You don't have to guess the number of jellybeans in a jar or bubbles on a bar of soap to register to vote. You don't have to risk your life to cast a ballot. Other people already did that for you. (Applause.) Your grandparents, your great grandparents might be here today if they were working on it. What's your excuse? When we don't vote, we give away our power, disenfranchise ourselves—right when we need to use the power that we have; right when we need your power to stop others from taking away the vote and rights of those more vulnerable than you are—the elderly and the poor, the formerly incarcerated trying to earn their second chance.

So you got to vote all the time, not just when it's cool, not just when it's time to elect a President, not just when you're inspired. It's your duty. When it's time to elect a member of Congress or a city councilman, or a school board member, or a sheriff. That's how we change our politics—by electing people at every level who are representative of and accountable to us. It is not that complicated. Don't make it complicated.

And finally, change requires more than just speaking out—it requires listening, as well. In particular, it requires listening to those with whom you disagree, and being prepared to compromise. When I was a state senator, I helped pass Illinois's first racial profiling law, and one of the first laws in the nation requiring the videotaping of confessions in capital cases. And we were successful because, early on, I engaged law enforcement. I didn't say to them, oh, you guys are so racist, you need to do something. I understood, as many of you do, that the overwhelming majority of police officers are good, and honest, and courageous, and fair, and love the communities they serve.

35   And we knew there were some bad apples, and that even the good cops with the best of intentions—including, by the way, African American police officers—might have unconscious biases, as we all do. So we engaged and we listened, and we kept working until we built consensus. And because we took the time to listen, we crafted legislation that was good for the police—because it improved the trust and cooperation of the community—and it was good for the communities, who were less likely to be treated unfairly. And I can say this unequivocally: without at least the acceptance of the police organizations in Illinois, I could never have gotten those bills passed. Very simple. They would have blocked them.

The point is, you need allies in a democracy. That's just the way it is. It can be frustrating and it can be slow. But history teaches us that the alternative to democracy is always worse. That's not just true in this country. It's not a black or white thing. Go to any country where the give and take of democracy has been repealed by one-party rule, and I will show you a country that does not work.

And democracy requires compromise, even when you are 100 percent right. This is hard to explain sometimes. You can be completely right, and you still are going to have to engage folks who disagree with you. If you think that the only way forward is to be as uncompromising as possible, you will feel good about yourself, you will enjoy a certain moral purity, but you're not going to get what you want. And if you don't get what you want long enough, you will eventually think the whole system is rigged. And that will lead to more cynicism, and less participation, and a downward spiral of more injustice and more anger and more despair. And that's never been the source of our progress. That's how we cheat ourselves of progress.

We remember Dr. King's soaring oratory, the power of his letter from a Birmingham jail, the marches he led. But he also sat down with President Johnson in the Oval Office to try and get a Civil Rights Act and a Voting Rights Act passed. And those two seminal bills were not perfect—just like the Emancipation Proclamation was a war document as much as it was some clarion call for freedom. Those mileposts of our progress were not perfect. They did not make up for centuries of slavery or Jim Crow or eliminate racism or provide for 40 acres and a mule. But they made things better. And you know what, I will take better every time. I always tell my staff—better is good, because you consolidate your gains and then you move on to the next fight from a stronger position.

Brittany Packnett, a member of the Black Lives Matter movement and Campaign Zero, one of the Ferguson protest organizers, she joined our Task Force on 21st Century Policing. Some of her fellow activists questioned whether she should participate. She rolled up her sleeves and sat at the same table with big city police chiefs and prosecutors. And because she did, she ended up shaping many of the recommendations of that task force. And those recommendations are now being adopted across the country—changes that many of the protesters called for. If young activists like Brittany had refused to participate out of some sense of ideological purity, then those great ideas would have just remained ideas. But she did participate. And that's how change happens.

40   America is big and it is boisterous and it is more diverse than ever. The president told me that we've got a significant Nepalese contingent here at Howard. I would not have guessed that. Right on. But it just tells you how interconnected we're becoming. And with so many folks from so many places, converging, we are not always going to agree with each other.

Another Howard alum, Zora Neale Hurston, once said — this is a good quote here: "Nothing that God ever made is the same thing to more than one person." Think about that. That's why our democracy gives us a process designed for us to settle our disputes with argument and ideas and votes instead of violence and simple majority rule.

So don't try to shut folks out, don't try to shut them down, no matter how much you might disagree with them. There's been a trend around the country of trying to get colleges to disinvite speakers with a different point of view, or disrupt a politician's rally. Don't do that — no matter how ridiculous or offensive you might find the things that come out of their mouths. Because as my grandmother used to tell me, every time a fool speaks, they are just advertising their own ignorance. Let them talk. Let them talk. If you don't, you just make them a victim, and then they can avoid accountability.

That doesn't mean you shouldn't challenge them. Have the confidence to challenge them, the confidence in the rightness of your position. There will be times when you shouldn't compromise your core values, your integrity, and you will have the responsibility to speak up in the face of injustice. But listen. Engage. If the other side has a point, learn from them. If they're wrong, rebut them. Teach them. Beat them on the battlefield of ideas. And you might as well start practicing now, because one thing I can guarantee you — you will have to deal with ignorance, hatred, racism, foolishness, trifling folks. (Laughter.) I promise you, you will have to deal with all that at every stage of your life. That may not seem fair, but life has never been completely fair. Nobody promised you a crystal stair. And if you want to make life fair, then you've got to start with the world as it is.

So that's my advice. That's how you change things. Change isn't something that happens every four years or eight years; change is not placing your faith in any particular politician and then just putting your feet up and saying, okay, go. Change is the effort of committed citizens who hitch their wagons to something bigger than themselves and fight for it every single day.

That's what Thurgood Marshall understood—a man who gradu-   45
ated from Howard Law, went home to Baltimore, and started his own law practice. He and his mentor, Charles Hamilton Houston, rolled up their sleeves and they set out to overturn segregation. They worked through the NAACP. Filed dozens of lawsuits, fought dozens of cas-es. And after nearly twenty years of effort—twenty years—Thurgood Marshall ultimately succeeded in bringing his righteous cause before the Supreme Court, and securing the ruling in Brown v. Board of Ed-ucation that separate could never be equal. (Applause.) Twenty years.

Marshall, Houston—they knew it would not be easy. They knew it would not be quick. They knew all sorts of obstacles would stand in their way. They knew that even if they won, that would just be the beginning of a longer march to equality. But they had discipline. They had persistence. They had faith—and a sense of humor. And they made life better for all Americans.

And I know you graduates share those qualities. I know it be-cause I've learned about some of the young people graduating here today. There's a young woman named Ciearra Jefferson, who's gradu-ating with you. And I'm just going to use her as an example. I hope you don't mind, Ciearra. Ciearra grew up in Detroit and was raised by a poor single mom who worked seven days a week in an auto plant. And for a time, her family found themselves without a place to call home. They bounced around between friends and family who might take them in. By her senior year, Ciearra was up at 5:00 am every day, juggling homework, extracurricular activities, volunteering, all while taking care of her little sister. But she knew that education was her ticket to a better life. So she never gave up. Pushed herself to excel. This daughter of a single mom who works on the assembly line turned down a full scholarship to Harvard to come to Howard. (Applause.)

And today, like many of you, Ciearra is the first in her family to graduate from college. And then, she says, she's going to go back to her hometown, just like Thurgood Marshall did, to make sure all the working folks she grew up with have access to the health care they need and deserve. As she puts it, she's going to be a "change agent." She's going to reach back and help folks like her succeed.

And people like Ciearra are why I remain optimistic about America. (Applause.) Young people like you are why I never give in to despair.

50   James Baldwin once wrote, "Not everything that is faced can be changed, but nothing can be changed until it is faced."

Graduates, each of us is only here because someone else faced down challenges for us. We are only who we are because someone else struggled and sacrificed for us. That's not just Thurgood Marshall's story, or Ciearra's story, or my story, or your story—that is the story of America. A story whispered by slaves in the cotton fields, the song of marchers in Selma, the dream of a King in the shadow of Lincoln. The prayer of immigrants who set out for a new world. The roar of women demanding the vote. The rallying cry of workers who built

America. And the GIs who bled overseas for our freedom.

Now it's your turn. And the good news is, you're ready. And when your journey seems too hard, and when you run into a chorus of cynics who tell you that you're being foolish to keep believing or that you can't do something, or that you should just give up, or you should just settle—you might say to yourself a little phrase that I've found handy these last eight years: yes, we can.

Congratulations, Class of 2016! (Applause.) Good luck! God bless you. God bless the United States of America. I'm proud of you.

I Just Got Called Racist, What Do I Do Now?

Ijeoma Oluo

Seattle author and speaker Ijeoma Oluo was named one of 2017s Most Influential People in Seattle by Seattle Magazine, *and is winner of the 2018 Feminist Humanist Award from the American Humanist Society. This piece is excerpted from her book* So You Want to Talk about Race.

"It was one of the most disgusting moments of my presidency," George W. Bush declared earnestly to Matt Lauer. Two years after his presidency, during which he started two wars that cost hundreds of thousands of lives and destabilized an entire region of the world, the former president was talking about the moments that had stood out to him. And there, in his list of "the most disgusting moments" was the time that Kanye West said that George W. Bush doesn't care about black people.

In his book *Decision Points*, Bush talks further about how hurt he was by Kanye's accusation. It was, in his words, an all-time low of his presidency: "I faced a lot of criticism as president. I didn't like hearing people claim that I lied about Iraq's weapons of mass destruction or cut taxes to benefit the rich. But the suggestion that I was racist because of the response to Katrina represented an all-time low."

I remember at the time feeling shocked and a little amused by this. After all the atrocities that George W. Bush saw in his presidency (terror attacks, unjust wars resulting in hundreds of thousands of deaths, the largest recession since the great depression, and so much more) having someone insinuate that he was racist was the all-time low. How out-of-touch. How self-centered. I remember thinking that it was yet another sign that the former president was a weird emotional child who was not at all qualified for the presidency (this was, of course, before Donald Trump showed us all what "weird, emotional child not at all qualified for the presidency" really looks like). But I thought of this mostly as a funny aberration.

That was, of course, until I started writing about race.

If you write about race or talk about race, you will quickly realize that GWB's reaction to the insinuation of racism is disturbingly common. To many white people, it appears, there is absolutely nothing worse than being called a racist, or someone insinuating you might be racist, or someone saying that something you did was racist, or somebody calling somebody you identify with racist. Basically, anytime the label of racist touches you at all, it's the worst thing to happen to anybody anywhere.

I remember once after sharing an article on Twitter about racism in the US, when a white Canadian tweeted back, "You should move to Canada, we aren't racist here." I pointed out that, according to recent news of the reluctance of government officials to fully investigate the murders of dozens of indigenous women, the controversy over "carding" of black Canadians by police, and the testimony of my Canadian friends of color—Canada was plenty racist. This white Canadian stranger kept insisting that no, there was no racism in Canada because he had not seen it. When some of my Canadian friends chimed in with helpful links about high-profile incidences of racism and investigations into systemic racism in Canada, the white Canadian continued to insist that they were wrong, and that racism doesn't exist in Canada.

I pointed out the irony of stating that racism doesn't exist, while talking over, belittling, and denying the lived experiences of Canadians of color.

His response was quick: "Are you calling me racist? YOU CUNT!"

Mr. Friendly White Canadian then proceeded to harass me on social media for weeks, until his account was suspended. For hours each day he sought out anyone who commented on one of my Tweets, informing them that I was a "reverse-racist" who "hated white people" and "loved calling innocent people racists." After I blocked him on Twitter, he would log on from other accounts he created just to continue the harassment. He did not appear to be, from his Internet history, a professional troll or serial harasser. Something about my insinuation that his actions may be racist had triggered a deep rage inside of him, and he was going to make me pay.

10   This is perhaps a slightly more extreme example of the racial confrontation formula: a white person does something racially insensitive and harmful, it is pointed out to them, and they go nuclear. People have tried to get me fired from gigs, have tried to organize protests of my public events, have sent me threatening emails—all for pointing out how their actions are hurting others.

And I'm not alone. When I asked a group of people of color what they feared most when talking about racism, their number-one concern was retaliation. One friend knows of at least two websites dedicated to smearing her because she called a white woman's language racist. One friend was fired from a job after a Facebook argument in which she said an associate was acting racist. One friend was subject to a months-long campaign to turn her community against her after stating that someone's actions were insensitive to people of color. Countless friends have had emails sent to their employers and educators by white people incensed that someone would insinuate that their actions are racist.

Even when the words "racist" or "racism" are never said—even the slightest implication can shift the entire conversation from "Hey, this hurts people of color" to "DID YOU JUST CALL ME RACIST? I AM NOT RACIST! I AM A GOOD PERSON! HOW DARE YOU?"

It's not as if it's easy for people of color to call out racism. When we decide to talk about these things, not only are we having to confront our own feelings of hurt, disappointment, or anger, we know that we are also risking any of the above reactions and more. When we decide to talk about racism, we know that it could indeed end our friendships, our reputations, our careers, and even our lives. The response to our complaints of racism or racial insensitivity are not always met with such violent reactions, but no matter what, it is never a pleasant conversation for people of color to have. I do not know a single person of color who does not broach these conversations with a very heavy heart, and they almost always leave with one even heavier.

So why do we talk about racism if it's so risky and so painful?

Because we have no choice. Because not talking about it is killing us. Because for far too long, the burden of racism has always been on us alone. If you are white, and you are reading this and wondering why we bother if these conversations are as bad as I say, think of how bad the alternative—continued, unchecked racism—would have to be in order to get you to risk that much, and you'll know a little more about the reality of life for people of color.

This chapter is for white people. Of course, non-white people will read it as well, and I hope that it is informative to most and perhaps validating to others. But I am aiming this chapter at you, the white person who is afraid of being called racist. Who may well be avoiding further investing in the fight for racial justice because you know that one wrong move may have you labeled as a white supremacist. If you see even a little bit of yourself in this, you need to keep reading. If you

15

are convinced that you are past all of that, you should probably still keep reading — because these defensive impulses run deep and may take you by surprise, just when you thought you had gotten past all of your discomfort around race.

Who are you?

You are, at times, kind and mean, generous and selfish, witty and dull. Sometimes you are all of these things at once.

And if you are white in a white supremacist society, you are racist. If you are male in a patriarchy, you are sexist. If you are able-bodied, you are ableist. If you are anything above poverty in a capitalist society, you are classist. You can sometimes be all of these things at once.

20   You do, as Walt Whitman said, contain multitudes.

I know that the above is all that some people need to chuck this book out a window. "Typical," some might say, "Another Social Justice Warrior who thinks all white people are racist." But you've come this far and already invested so much in this process — please, consider sitting with your discomfort for a while longer, and see where this chapter takes you.

We like to think of our character in the same way it is written in our obituaries. We are strong, brave, and loyal. We are funny and creative. We are what we strive to be. While if we sit and reflect, we can provide a more nuanced description of ourselves, in our day-to-day lives our self-esteem reads in synopsis: "Mary was a kind and loving mother. An avid gardener."

But life is a series of moments. And in reality we are both the culmination of those countless moments, and each moment individually in time.

Say you get drunk in a bar and punch a stranger in the face, spend the night in jail, realize that your life has taken a turn for the worse, get treatment, stop drinking, and dedicate your life to anti-violence work. To the person that you punched that night, you may forever be the person who assaulted them. The person who made them scared to go into bars for a while. The person who made them feel violated. To the people you have helped since, you may always be a hero. The person who made them safer in the world.

These are both who you are, they are both valid and do not cancel each other out. If you run into the person you punched years later, they may well still be afraid of you, they may react with anger. They will treat you like someone who punched them, because you are. And even if you respond to that anger and fear like someone who abhors violence, because that is also who you are, you have no right to demand that they see you differently.

Why all of this talk about the ways in which we can all be both an abuser and a healer? Because you have been racist, and you have been anti-racist. Yes, you may now be insisting that you do not have a racist bone in your body, but that is simply not true. You have been racist, and will be in the future, even if less so.

You are racist because you were born and bred in a racist, white supremacist society. White Supremacy is, as I've said earlier, insidious by design. The racism required to uphold White Supremacy is woven into every area of our lives. There is no way you can inherit white privilege from birth, learn racist white supremacist history in schools, consume racist and white supremacist movies and films, work in a racist and white supremacist workforce, and vote for racist and white supremacist governments and not be racist.

This does not mean that you have hate in your heart. You may intend to treat everyone equally. But it does mean that you have absorbed some fucked-up shit regarding race, and it will show itself in some fucked-up ways. You may not know why you clutch your purse a little harder when a black man walks by you, but in the moment you do, you are being racist. You may not know why when you see a bad driver on the road and you recognize they are Asian a little voice inside you goes "Aha!" but in that moment, you are being racist. You may not know why you are pleasantly surprised that the Latinx person you are talking to is "so articulate" but in that moment, you are being racist.

And that racism informs a lot of your decisions in ways that you are not aware. It informs how you vote, where you spend your money, whom you hire, what books you read, whom you socialize with, what social concerns you will pay attention to. And that racism does real harm to real people, both immediately and systematically. To the person you harmed in that racist moment, you may forever be the person who harmed them, because you did. You may also be other things to them—you may also be a friend, a coworker, or a neighbor. And you can decide that you don't ever want to be a racist to anyone else, and you can work toward that goal, but you cannot tell someone to deny the harm you've done to them.

30   And that sucks. It sucks to know that to some people you will forever be the person who harmed them. It sucks to know that someone you have harmed in the past may one day read in your obituary "John was a generous and loyal friend to all he met" and disagree. You've tried so hard to be a good person, but your intentions cannot erase the harm that your actions cause.

This is real harm that has been done and you have to accept that if you do not want to continue harming people by denying their lived experiences and denying your responsibility. This does not mean that you have to flog yourself for all eternity. The pain you've caused is real, and if you have a conscience, the recognition of that will likely sting a little whenever you think about it. But everything else you've done, all of the effort you've made to be a better person, that is just as valid and deserves equal billing in your obit. Your mistakes or your achievements will never on their own define you. But you can only do better if you are willing to look at your entire self.

All of this is to say that if you have been called racist, or something you have done has been called racist by a person of color, you cannot simply dismiss it outright — even if that accusation is in direct opposition to all that you try to be. Not if you are truly committed to racial justice.

Now is an opportunity to learn more about yourself, to see yourself and your actions more clearly, so you can move toward the person you truly want to be. The question is: do you want to *look* like a better person, or do you want to *be* a better person? Because those who just want to look like a better person will have great difficulty with the introspection necessary to actually be a better person. In order to do better we must be willing to hold our darkness to the light, we must be willing to shatter our own veneer of "goodness."

So if you've been confronted with the possibility of your own racism, and you want to *do the work*, here are some tips:

> **Listen**. First and foremost, if someone is telling you something about yourself and your actions and you feel your hackles raising, take that as a sign that you need to stop and listen. If your blood pressure rose too quickly to really hear what was being said, take a few deep breaths, ask the person to repeat themselves if necessary, and listen again. Don't add to what the person is saying, don't jump to conclusions, don't immediately think "Oh you think I'm a monster now," just try to actually hear what they are trying to communicate to you.

> **Set your intentions aside**. Your intentions have little to no impact on the way in which your actions may have harmed

others. Do not try to absolve yourself of responsibility with your good intentions.

Try to hear the impact of what you have done. Don't just hear the action: "You consistently speak over me in work meetings and you do not do that to white people in our meetings." That is easy to brush off as, "I just didn't agree with you," or, "I didn't mean to, I was just excited about a point I was trying to make. Don't make a big deal out of nothing." Try to also hear the impact: "Your bias is invalidating my professional expertise and making me feel singled out and unappreciated in a way which compounds all of the many ways I'm made to feel this way as a woman of color in the workplace."

Remember that you do not have all of the pieces. You are not living as a person of color. You will never fully understand the impact that sustained, systemic racism has on people of color. You will never be able to fully empathize with the pain your actions may have caused. Nothing will get you there. Do not discount someone's complaint because their emotions seem foreign to you. You may think that someone is making a mountain out of a molehill, but when it comes to race, actual mountains are indeed made of countless molehills stacked on top of each other. Each one adds to the enormity of the problem of racism.

Nobody owes you a debate. It is very hard on people of color to call out racism. Sometimes, that is the most they can do. And while you may really want to get it all sorted out right then and there, understand that when you ask to "talk it out" you are asking for more emotional labor from somebody who is already hurt. It is nice if you get it, and you should be grateful, but it is not owed you. You can still give this serious thought. You can still look deep inside yourself, you can still Google for more insight (remember, it's highly unlikely that anything you've done has not been done before), even if the person who brought this to your attention does not want to engage further.

Nobody owes you a relationship. Even if you've recognized where you've been racist, worked to make amends, and learned from your mistakes, the person that you harmed does not owe you a relationship of any kind. In a hostile world, people of color have the right to cut off contact with people who have harmed them. They do not have to stick around to see all the progress you've made.

Remember that you are not the only one hurt. Yes, it hurts to know that somebody thinks you are being racist. But you were not the first one hurt here — it is the deep hurt of racism that forced this person to confront you. Do not make this about your pain at being called out.

If you can see where you have been racist, or if you can see where your actions have caused harm, apologize and mean it. Think about how you can make amends if possible, and how you can avoid those same harmful actions in the future. If you cannot see where you have been racist, take some more rime to seriously consider the issue some more before declaring your actions "not racist." There have been conversations I've had about race with white people that ended in absolute denials, only to have that white person come back to me months later to say that they finally realized that their actions were racist and they were sorry for the harm they had caused, not only by their actions, but by their vigorous denial of my experiences.

If, after a lot of careful thought, you still do not see your actions as racist and feel strongly that this is simply a misunderstanding, do not then invalidate that person's hurt. A true misunderstanding isn't so just because your intentions were not racist. A true misunderstanding is when your actions do not actually have a racist impact even though somebody thinks they might. If I hit you but do not intend to hit you, that is not a misunderstanding about whether or not I hit you. The situation you are in may be a misunderstanding—it does happen, even if it happens less often than you think. But even if it is, the pain of the person confronting you is real. Do not deny that. Do not call it silly. Explain your viewpoint if you feel it's necessary, and hope that explanation sheds light that helps that person see the situation the same way that you do, but don't deny someone's lived experience. Your goal is to find out if you are being racist, not to prove that you aren't, and to resolve a painful situation if possible.

35   This is not an easy process, and it is not at all fun. And at times, it seems never-ending. At times it may seem like no matter what you do, you are doing something wrong. But you have to try to adjust to the feelings of shame and pain that come from being confronted with your own racism. You have to get over the fear of facing the worst in yourself. You should instead fear unexamined racism. Fear the thought that right now, you could be contributing to the oppression of others and you don't know it. But do not fear those who bring that oppression to light. Do not fear the opportunity to do better.

Bread and Roses

James Oppenheim

James Oppenheim (1882–1932) was a poet, writer of short stories and novels, and editor whose work largely focused on psychology and labor rights. The bread and roses in his poem come from a speech by Rose Schneiderman: "The worker must have bread, but she must have roses, too." Oppenheim's poem was first published in The American Magazine *in 1911. It was later set to music and became an anthem for workers' rights.*

As we come marching, marching in the beauty of the day,
A million darkened kitchens, a thousand mill-lofts gray
Are touched with all the radiance that a sudden sun discloses,
For the people hear us singing, "Bread and Roses, Bread and Roses."

As we come marching, marching, we battle, too, for men —
For they are women's children and we mother them again.
Our lives shall not be sweated from birth until life closes —
Hearts starve as well as bodies: Give us Bread, but give us Roses.

As we come marching, marching, unnumbered women dead
Go crying through our singing their ancient call for Bread;
Small art and love and beauty their drudging spirits knew —
Yes, it is Bread we fight for — but we fight for Roses, too.

As we come marching, marching, we bring the Greater Days —
The rising of the women means the rising of the race —
No more the drudge and idler — ten that toil where one
reposes —
But a sharing of life's glories: Bread and Roses, Bread and Roses.

Roots & Wings
A Memoir of Hope and Transformation
Demetra Perros

Demetra Perros is a writer, performer, and teacher. This excerpt is from her book and one-woman show, Roots & Wings. *She lives in Montana with her family.*

What suffering must you endure?
Euripides, *Hekebe*

Why do certain people develop post-traumatic stress disorder while others do not? This question has plagued me for years. One prominent theory explaining why certain people develop PTSD has less to do with the event itself, and more to do with their return to everyday life. Even after traumatic events that don't take place abroad or away from home, such as domestic violence or molestation, there is an attempted return to what was once familiar. The manner in which people are received by their peers and communities post-event plays a crucial role in their recovery from trauma.

Take World War II veterans, for example. When soldiers returned home, generally speaking, they were welcomed back as heroes. Parades were held in their honor, and trees were draped with yellow ribbons. They had fought "The Good War." But when soldiers returned from Vietnam, there were few open arms and fewer celebrations. They had fought in a war that divided a nation. They had fought amid home front protests. They did not experience a welcome homecoming. With the recent return of soldiers from Iraq, Afghanistan, and other war-torn regions, it is imperative that they feel they are being welcomed home. Their recovery may hinge upon it.

In a study examining former Nepalese child soldiers, medical anthropologist Brandon Kohrt, MD and PhD, observed the influence returning to one's former environment has on trauma recovery. In the *New York Times* article "A New Focus on the 'Post' in Post-Traumatic Stress," author David Dobbs writes about Dr. Kohrt's research: Every child "experienced violence and other events considered traumatic . . . Yet their postwar mental health depended not on their exposure to war but on how their families and villages received them." Dr. Kohrt found that children whose villages welcomed them home with rituals or acts of reintegration suffered minimal effects of trauma. The same did not hold true for those who received little support from their communities upon returning home. Dobbs writes, "In villages where the children were stigmatized or ostracized, they suffered high, persistent levels of post-traumatic stress disorder." Based on my own experience, I, too, believe the homecoming is equally — if not more — influential than a history of past trauma.

When I returned, I was not reintegrated into my high school community. The administration's reluctance to reinstate my valedictorian status, not to mention its debate about whether or not I could even graduate, negatively impacted the condition of my return. To an honor student, your work is your identity, and if your hard work is not being acknowledged, then neither are you.

Very little is needed to make someone feel welcomed: Glad to see you. Glad you're back. A hug. That's all it takes.

After recuperating at home, I drove myself to high school. With no explanation, I reappeared in class, like a familiar stranger. Mrs. Presley was the only teacher I remember who welcomed me back. She taught a fiction elective my senior year. I had taken her class fall semester, and when I returned, it was the only elective other than choir that I continued taking.

"Joining us from last semester is Jamie," she told the students.

I was sitting in a row near her desk, looking down at my oversized water bottle.

10   "We're very glad to have her here, with us."

In her welcoming, I heard an acknowledgement of the seriousness of my health condition. She was thankful not just that I had returned to class, but that I had come back at all.

The students in that class never asked me about the ship. I never felt like I had to justify or explain myself. I was able to move forward, if only in that room, because my peers had accepted my return.

While primary communities for teenagers include school and home, secondary communities include extracurricular activities like jobs, sports teams, and clubs. When I returned to high school, the student council kind of invited me back, and kind of didn't. I remember my vice president saying I should come to meetings, but I was never given information about where or when they were held. What was I supposed to do? Stalk the halls at lunchtime, peeking into classrooms to see where they were? Because I was not re-welcomed into this former community, I felt excluded. I believed the group that had once respected me didn't want me anymore. Maybe I looked as though I had moved past high school clubs.

But I hadn't.

15   As trivial as I think this sounds, not going back to some stupid high school student council still rips me up inside. Believe me, I wish it didn't. But here they are: the tears I never cried spring semester of my senior year because I was too shell-shocked to process emotion then.

I understand now that what I needed was to participate in the same activities I had before the event. Instead, I became separated from my classmates. It's hard to identify what came first, the isolation or the shame. Because I was isolated from former communities, I felt ashamed. Because I felt ashamed, I further isolated myself from what was once familiar and supportive.

In retrospect, it's easier to identify communities that could've helped me reintegrate back into high school. I think the community that had the most potential to offer support was my choir, a group of sixteen young women, many of whom performed at Grandstreet The-atre too. We were a tight-knit group, and eventually we created what we called "Circle Time." Sitting on the tile floor of the choir room, we confided in each other about crushes, breakups, and other stresses in our teenage lives. Circle Time was a nonjudgmental, confidential space where we could share whatever we felt. Even our conductor, Mr. Williams, valued Circle Time. He saw it as a bonding activity that strengthened his singers' ability to harmonize and blend as a cohesive ensemble. If we rehearsed well, he often gave us the last ten minutes of class to have Circle Time while he went into his office to prepare for his other choirs, always shutting the door to give us privacy. The girls had been with me through the application process for Oceans Abroad, and they'd thrown a farewell party for me before I left for the Philippines.

The day I returned to choir, I pulled up a chair at my old spot, next to Samantha in the alto section. As the girls trickled in, they noticed me and rushed over, asking if I was okay. I remember feeling overwhelmed by their bombardment of concern. Luckily, the choir president motioned to form a circle. As we were setting our music folders down and gathering on the floor, Mr. Williams walked out of his office.

"Time to rehearse," he said. "We have a lot to do this week."

20   I could tell that the girls were torn between obeying their teacher and supporting their friend. "But Jamie just got back!" one of them argued.

"If there's time afterward, you can have Circle Time," Mr. Williams said.

We rehearsed until the bell rang.

The choir was preparing for an upcoming competition. That weekend, the group was traveling to Spokane, a six-hour bus ride away. I felt wary of traveling so soon after Oceans Abroad. My parents, and even Dr. Pitney, advised against going on the trip. I remember feeling relieved I had a doctor's note to explain why I couldn't go.

With our intensive rehearsals that week, we never had a chance for Circle Time. When the girls returned from Spokane, I felt left out by their references and jokes. Any chance of confiding in them had passed.

25   I see now that going on the choir trip could've offered a chance for me to talk about my experience with my peers. It could've helped me begin to process my emotions and soften my critical mind. I've imagined the dim light of a hotel room with the fifteen girls lounging on beds and hugging pillows as they listened to my story, siding with me when the ship staff insisted I was fine, and consoling me when I shared that I felt like I had let everyone down, including them.

Unfortunately, that never happened.

I wish I could have traded a farewell party for a welcome home party, which is, in itself, an act of reintegration. Before leaving for Oceans Abroad, my friends and family threw me not one, but three farewell parties: the intimate choir party, a huge surprise party attended by high school and Grandstreet Theatre friends and alumni, and a family party of my favorite Greek foods. When I returned from Cambodia, blistered and emaciated, no welcome home parties were thrown.

Nor was there any event that celebrated my return. Why would there have been? None of us knew how integral the homecoming phase is for trauma survivors. None of us even knew I had endured trauma. After decades, our nation is only beginning to recognize the role the post-event environment plays in saving people from social isolation.

The Terrible Things
I Learned About My Dad
On Abuse and the People We Love

Liz Prato

Liz Prato is a writer, editor, and teacher living in Portland. Her essay, first published in 2015, recalls cleaning out her father's house after his death and finding many disturbing things, including evidence that he had molested Prato's troubled brother, who died a year later. Prato—who worked for a time answering phones at an organization dedicated to the prevention of child abuse, and heard harrowing, graphic stories from adult survivors—struggles with how to reconcile these new terrible facts with her memory of the father she loved.

These are some of the things I found when cleaning out my dad's house after he died: his rainbow of karate belts and black belt certificates (1st and 2nd degree), a framed picture of us dancing together at a black-tie gala, the 387 type-written pages of his memoir, one 3 x 5 index card and one small square of paper etched with his handwriting, and almost a hundred letters from women my dad met on www.russianbrides.com.

My dad had been corresponding with—and in some cases, actually meeting—the Russian women for thirteen years. I don't know if he was looking for love, or just sex, or something more enigmatic (as if love and sex are so simple). In my dad's four-thousand-square-foot house in Denver, I found dozens of file folders and binders containing hundreds of webpage printouts featuring a woman's picture, her name, her height and weight, her location, maybe her profession, and her catalogue number. I found receipts from Western Union, showing my dad had wired money to several women — $200 here, $150 there — and sent gifts from Victoria's Secret. I found nearly a hundred letters written to him on wispy airmail paper and accompanied by photos: some simple headshots, many garish poses intended to look sexy, and a few so dour that you'd have to wonder not just about the sorrows of the woman pictured, but the sorrows of any man who would look at the photo and say, "That's the mate for me."

Nothing about my dad, my exterior dad — the son of poor Italian immigrants who was a rags-to-riches story, buying up barren parcels of land near highway interchanges in the Sixties and then selling them to gas stations and hotels and Stuckey's, my exterior dad with a big, bright smile that made you feel like nothing had ever made him happier than you just walking in the door — would make you think he was desperate or pathetic or lonely. My parents divorced when he was in his early fifties and my dad always had female companions — he was a good-looking enough guy, and friendly, and liked to spoil the women in his life (myself included). However, when I was a teenager, I found stacks of letters from women responding to his personal ads in The Denver Post and The Rocky Mountain News. So, there was precedent, sort of, for his correspondence with the Russian wannabe-brides.

When I cleaned out his house, I also found copies of my dad's own letters to the Russians. On one day he sent the same introductory letter to nineteen different women. He fudged the facts of his age — claiming to be 65, even though he was 70 — and his interests — professing a deep love for literature, even though his real-life library had that Gatsby-esque quality of being populated by unopened volumes — and his marital status. My parents had already been divorced for fourteen years when my mom died, but my dad told all these women, "My wife of many years died several years ago. Only in the last two years have I begun to consider a new life with a new partner." In fact, since he and my mom split, my dad had been with many women (see above: personal ads), some who I knew, and some who I found out about because their names were on his list of people he'd had sex with.

5   I didn't actually find The List while cleaning out my dad's house. I found it four years after he died, in the cardboard box marked "Russians" stored in my garage in Portland. I'd saved these odd artifacts to and from the Russian women, thinking someday I would write a funny and insightful essay about this predilection of my dad's, hoping they would help me understand something about those women and my own father and, maybe, something about the human heart and the ways in which we get broken then try to get unbroken again. That's why I was going through the cardboard box of letters and photographs, when I unexpectedly found The List.

It was a sheet of white paper on which my dad had hand-written two columns of women's names: his first girlfriend, a woman he almost married, my mom, several women he dated after they divorced who I knew, a handful of Russian names—some he'd mentioned to me, others who he had not. I didn't know every name on the list, and, more disturbingly, neither did he: Girl in Boulder; Girl at Congress Park; Girl on Marion Street; Mexican Girl.

My husband assured me that the word "girl" was just generational, the way all women were once referred to as girls by men who wore hats to work and enjoyed a stiff drink when they came home. Still, it was not entirely reassuring that my dad was meeting—and quite possibly cruising—women in these random places.

And then, at the bottom of the list, my dad had written: "(over)." As in "turn over." As in "this list continues on the other side." So, I turned the list over. There were only two names on the other side. One I didn't know, and one I did. My brother. Steve.

These are the things I already knew, before my dad died, and before my brother died a year later: My dad was a narcissist. He could not care about anything unless it was directly related to one of his various obsessions: The sinking of the S.S. Franklin in WWII, Notre Dame football, Jungian psychology, some quack in Missouri who claimed he could cure any ailment with some questionable contraption, and my brother, Steve. Steve was an alcoholic and lived at home and worked for our dad his entire adult life. My dad was obsessed with "how to fix Steve," a project which started requiring more attention when Steve began drinking around age 15. "Fixing Steve" involved, among other things, buying Steve a three-bedroom condo across the street from the bar he frequented—so he wouldn't get behind the wheel of a car—and continuing to pay for it for a good three years, even though Steve never moved in. It involved writing letters to Steve's therapist to suggest what she should and should not do with him after Steve's divorce. His obsession involved being so petrified that Steve might die at age 43 if he had both his hips replaced—which he desperately needed, because avascular necrosis had destroyed his joints—that he encouraged Steve to try "alternative therapies" (see above: quack's contraption) instead of surgery. The avascular necrosis may have been caused by Steve's drinking, and it may have been caused by his years as a young athlete, and it may have been some unpredictable alchemy of his DNA. Whatever the source, it left Steve in too much pain to even sit upright, much less stand or walk. My brother laid flat in bed for eighteen months and became addicted to morphine and Xanax and Ambien, and died of two pulmonary emboli at four in the morning when he was forty-five years old, a year after my dad died.

I also knew that Steve was diagnosed as bipolar when he was 40, but our dad convinced him to stop taking the lithium, saying, "Those   10 doctors are wrong, and whatever this is we'll beat it with willpower." That's how badly he hated the stigma of a mentally ill son; he thought he could just make it disappear by deciding it was untrue. These are the things I knew.

And I always knew this: My dad loved me and Steve, and tried to give us a good life with a stable home and good schools and Hawaiian vacations and telling us he loved us all the time, the kind of life he did not have as the child of a poor, abusive, alcoholic, immigrant father.

It had never, in my most repulsive nightmares, occurred to me that my dad might have molested my brother. I believed their unfixable, codependent-isn't-even-a-big-enough-word relationship was about addiction and guilt and mental illness and hubris and narcissism. No other explanation was needed. When I read Steve's name on that list while standing in my study with the Russians at my feet, everything froze: the air, my blood, my breath, my brain. I felt it was true. I believed it was true. And I wasn't even remotely ready for it to be true.

I remembered something else I found, four years earlier, when I cleaned out my dad's house in Denver: One 2 x 2 piece of paper with my dad's handwriting on it that said:

Pedophilia – sexual abuse
Frotteurism – rubbing against a non consenting

And a 3 x 5 index card scarred by my dad's handwriting:

Vitiate: debase, pervert
        Make legally without force
        invalidate

15   In his four thousand square foot house there were hundreds of scraps of paper. Hundreds of files, hundreds of books, dozens of bind-

ers, birth certificates and marriage certificates and death certificates for aunts and uncles and my mother and father and brother, and I had four days to decide what to keep or throw away or sell. I did not have time to stop and get interested in or sentimental about what I found. But when I discovered the square piece of paper and the index card, I stopped. I stopped moving, stopped thinking about what had to be done, stopped trying to not think about my whole family being dead, and if it was really possible for one's heart to stop . . . it would have happened right then. Because those two scraps of paper were weighted with those two words: pedophilia. Pervert. I put them in an envelope that I did not store in a box in my garage in Portland, but kept in my desk, just in case I ever needed them.

Only a few days after I discovered The List, I unearthed the envelope containing the square paper and the index card. Pedophilia. Frotteurism. I set them on my desk next to The List, and it was instantly obvious how they fit together. Like pieces of a puzzle. Not a complete picture—the center few pieces still missing—but more than just edges. More than a border without a middle.

Something else I found in my dad's house: the type-written pages of his memoir. It was tucked in a brown accordion file folder in the basement, on the bottom shelf of a bookcase. He'd written it twenty years before he died, when he was 63. In those twenty years, he'd also written and self-published a book of poetry, a handbook of financial advice for women, and an historical novel based on the rescue of the USS. Franklin. He was proud of his books and was even fervently trying to get the novel made into a movie. I had never heard one word about his memoir.

Like most of my father's belongings that I did not sell or throw away, his memoir was stored in a box in my garage. After looking at that not-quite-complete puzzle on my desk, I retrieved the memoir and sped-read through it on my bed. I didn't think there'd be any admission of my father molesting my brother in those pages, but maybe there'd be some clue about how my dad became that kind of man. I thought I'd find proof that a Catholic priest had molested him when he was an altar boy, but my dad only wrote high praise for the padre who took him under his wing. Maybe there was some other man—an uncle or grandfather or even his father—who had sexually abused my dad, and he had been unable to break the cycle. But no. There was no evidence of such a defense.

However, there was reams of sadness and loss of a desolate quality that reached beyond his family's poverty. My namesake great-grandmother, Elizabeth, had come over from Italy to the tiny mining town of Aguilar, Colorado, leaving her two sons behind. My great-grandfather did not accompany her and no one in my family knows why; he had apparently done something so horrendous that it was literally unspeakable. When she first arrived in Aguilar, Elizabeth made money by "singing and dancing for the miners in a local bar." My dad provided no more details in his memoir and perhaps he knew none, but my mind goes to prurient places. She met and married the man who my dad came to know as his Grandfather, and sent for her two sons in Italy. It's a melancholy sepia photo in my brain, of my twelve year-old grandfather and his older brother alone on a ship, all the way from Italy to Ellis Island, and then somehow to a hamlet in Southern Colorado. My grandfather dropped out of school to help Elizabeth and his new father run a small grocery store. His brother fought in WWI, then died in 1922 of pneumonia. My grandfather met my grandmother, and along came my dad and his sister.

20   I was skimming through this part of my dad's memoir, because it seemed like facts, and I was looking for truths. My dad recounted several stories from his childhood (being verbally and physically abused

by his dad, climbing a local mountain by himself, losing his virginity), but what loomed large was the omnipresence of death. The backdrop was one of those perfect metaphors that you can't make up because it seems too forced, too conveniently placed. As part of running the grocery store, my grandfather and great-grandfather butchered cattle and hogs in a slaughterhouse behind their house. My dad would watch the animals go in alive, then come out dead, blood soaking their carcass and the ground.

When my dad was 8, Elizabeth—his protector from his abusive father—died of some unnamed illness. Less than a year later my dad's grandfather died, as a result of a car accident caused by a violent fight between the three people in the car (the other two survived). My dad himself almost succumbed to Scarlet Fever, although it was not clear at what age. He fell into a coma and last rites were administered, but somehow, two days later, he woke up and survived. When my dad was 12, his father was fatally felled by strep. Next, his cousin died of rheumatic fever, and six months later my dad's godfather died. Then went both his maternal grandparents and his uncle. It was all capped off when my dad's mother tried to (unsuccessfully) kill herself with an overdose of pills. This was all before my dad turned 18.

"What's wrong with my family?" he started asking. "Is God against us?"

"What's wrong with my family? I had asked so many times. Addiction and guilt and mental illness and hubris and narcissism, and I felt my own special inheritance was the one of loss. My mom, dad, brother, aunts, uncles—even friends—dead. My dad's mother died before I was born, and his sister died when I was 18. My dad knew what it was like to be the only survivor of a legacy of loss. At 18, I had no idea what that meant to him. I'm not even sure I know now, at 47, with my mom and dad and brother gone, and me holding The List and those pieces of paper and the 387-page memoir.

There were no admissions of my dad being molested in those pages. He graduated from high school and served in the South Pacific at the end of WWII and went to college in Boulder, and he wrote about how badly he struggled to escape where he came from. It was hard for him to study philosophy and psychology with middle class men and women, when no one in his family had ever even graduated from high school, when none of the women he'd grown up with were educated or independent.

25   My dad met a woman in a philosophy class that he would take to Denver for dinner sometimes. "She was looking for a kind of intimacy that I didn't understand and was still incapable of," my dad wrote. "I was looking for a piece of ass. One night parked in front of her house, I managed to pull down her panties and have sex with her despite her struggling against me. My experience was that when a woman said no, she was just being coy. For me that struggle was just a way to say yes. For her it was devastating. Today people would call it date rape."

He then wrote that his next "relationship" ended the same way.

My dad date raped two women — that he admits to. It would be easy (would it?) to excuse his actions by saying that men in his generation didn't know better, since date rape was not a thing people thought about, talked about, even had a definition for back then. I'm also well aware that in 1950 not every young man with a woman in his car thought it was his right to have sex with her, regardless of how much she struggled or said no. My dad wrote that "for her it was devastating," but he did not indicate it had been devastating for him, decades later, when he realized what he had done and had the word "rape" to attach to it. He did not profess to guilt or shame or an inner torment about his actions; he merely used it as an example of the kind of man he once was. I think he assumed the implication was he was no longer that man, that he would never fathom violating another human being, again. But he never wrote that, or anything close to it. Not once.

It makes me wonder about the Girl in Boulder, Girl at Congress Park, Girl on Marion Street, Mexican Girl. Were these casual, but consensual, sexual encounters with women whose names he did not remember? Or did he give these women no names because the way he had sex with them required them to be less than human?

After I found The List and the small pieces of paper and the memoir, I told only a handful of people what I had thought I had discovered. What I suspected, what I knew. I was not ready to be that person, the person whose dad was a sexual predator. I was not ready for it to be part of my story. I told my husband, my best friend, my brother's best friend, my therapist. And here's the thing: none of them tried to disabuse me of my conclusions. No one told me that I was misinterpreting, that there was some other explanation. No one tried to tell me my worst fears were wrong.

My friend Michelle and I met right after college when we were   30 working at a foundation that raised money for The Kempe Center for the Prevention and Treatment of Child Abuse and Neglect in Denver. Right after we started the job, the Kempe Center launched a new program researching the effects of childhood sexual abuse on adults. It was originally intended to be a small study with only twenty participants. They announced the new program in an auditorium at the University of Colorado Medical School, where a former Miss America from Denver stood up and, for the first time, publicly admitted that her father, a respected millionaire, had sexually abused her throughout her childhood.

That night over a hundred messages were left on the Foundation's answering machine, and all five lines of the phone were lit up for weeks. Some people called to express disgust over what they assumed were Miss America's vicious lies. But most of the calls were from adults who had been raped as children. Where can I get help?

Michelle and I were in charge of answering the phones. We were just the fundraising arm, we tried to explain. The Kempe Center, itself, was also inundated with calls, and was no more ready to deal with the tidal wave of injured souls. The most we could do was recommend help lines and therapists and support groups to the callers.

Sometimes, the callers didn't want a phone number. Sometimes, they needed to tell their story and launched into it as soon as they heard a human voice on the other end. Michelle and I heard ugliness and evil that we didn't know existed. Dr. Henry Kempe, the founder of the agency, used to say that most parents didn't mean to abuse their children. That they lacked certain resources—emotional, financial, etc.—and just snapped, but they were not evil. But I think Kempe was talking more about physical abuse, about hitting, slapping, shaking. Frustration, tempers, fear. Those were not the stories we heard when survivors recounted their own sexual abuses. One story remains forever lodged in both of our brains, about a girl whose father molested her with her own Barbie doll. Michelle and I were held hostage by these horrors, unable to hang up on someone in the midst of reliving such brutal trauma, but also untrained in how to help them or how to shield ourselves.

Somehow, Michelle was able to compartmentalize, but I broke out in hives—almost two hundred hives all over my body, including on my lips and the bottom of my feet—every day for six months. I changed laundry soap and I changed my diet. I endeavored to discover if I had some repressed memory of being sexually abused that was triggered by my job and causing these red, angry welts, but no shadowy memories took shape. Night after night I would get only a few hours of sleep—and that was with Benadryl—because I would wake up at one, two, three in the morning, scratching furiously. I went to an allergist (who made a note in the chart that I was "emotional") and the allergist found no substance that should be triggering such a dramatic response. He had no suggestions beyond that, and it felt like a failing on my part.

Six months after the hives appeared they mysteriously retreat- 35 ed, returning to me my smooth, calm skin. I'll never know if it was because my boss decided I didn't have to field survivor phone calls anymore, or because I dumped the abusive boyfriend I lived with, or because of some other secret that my body and mind had sequestered in its deepest functioning systems was pushed even deeper. Or maybe my body and mind just got exasperated with me for not figuring out what it was trying to tell me, and gave up.

Not long after the hives disappeared, my dad joined the board of the Kempe Foundation. The former Miss America's husband was an old business colleague of my dad's, and invited him to join. My dad was enormously proud to participate in and represent an organization that did such important work, and he wanted them to be proud of him being on their board. In the packet we handed out to each member at his first board meeting was his thirty-two page CV, which included newspaper clippings about his biggest business deals, a picture of him in his karate gi, and a statement of his net worth. I was embarrassed, but even then intrigued, about why he felt the need to go to such lengths to convince the other board members he was worthy. "You can take Pete out of Aguilar," a neighbor used to say, "But you can't take the Aguilar out of Pete." It was as if he was afraid these men and women of industry and society would be able to look at him and know, somehow, where he had come from.

After I was amicably laid off from my job, my dad bought two seats to the Foundation's fancy fundraising dinner. He wore a tuxedo with a crimson bow tie and I wore a little black dress with faux-pearls, and when we pulled up to valet parking in his Cadillac, I felt like royalty. We shared a table with people far above our social and financial station, people for whom I used to work, while my friend still at the Foundation — Michelle — made fun of me for being an attendee, and not a looked-down-upon worker bee.

That night someone snapped a picture of me and my dad, one of my favorite pictures, ever, and also my dad's. I found it in a pewter frame in his house. We were dancing together to a swing band — I was a terrible dancer, never having gone to cotillion and learned the steps, but my dad didn't seem to mind. He was in a tuxedo, and I was in a little black dress. We were both smiling. Happy.

When I told Michelle about The List and the index card and the square piece of paper, she just sighed out a long, "Ooooh." She did not try to tell me that I was wrong, that I'd misinterpreted, that I'd overreacted. She said, "This explains everything that was wrong with Steve."

"My dad was a monster," I whispered. "But you knew him . . . he wasn't."

"Liz, we know someone isn't just born as an abuser. Something happened to him. It's probably why he was so broken."

When I first looked through the cardboard box marked "Russians," I wanted to understand something about my dad, and these women, and hopefully something about the ways in which we are all broken and try to put the pieces back together, even in incredibly broken ways. I still don't know what is true, what is circumstantial, what my dad actually did and had done to him, and whether those hives were about the people I listened to, or about something that happened in my own family that I knew, on a cellular level, but couldn't face.

But I do know. Because when I first found my brother's name on

The List, I felt broken in a way that could not be fixed. I didn't think I could live with this knowledge. Everything inside me felt shredded, like my ribcage had been scraped raw.

My father was a monster.

The index card that said "Vitiate: debase, pervert/Make legally   45
without force/invalidate" was paper-clipped to a smaller piece of an index card. On the non-lined side, these words were typed:

> Hast not thy share
> On winged feet
> Lo it rushed thee to meet.
> And all that nature made they own
> Flowing in Air and pent in stone
> Will rive the hills and swim the sea
> And like they shadow follow thee.

I didn't know what these words meant when I found them, what they are from, although I assumed the Bible, because my dad believed in God and Christ. A Google search revealed they are from an Emerson poem preceding his essay, "Compensation." In "Compensation," Emerson asserts that just like there is polarity in every aspect of nature (light and dark, male and female, hot and cold, the systole and diastole of the heart), there is polarity within humans. "Every excess causes a defect; every defect an excess. Every sweet hath its sour; every evil its good."

A century(-ish) later, Carl Jung's followers used this poem and essay to support the theory of the "shadow self"—the part of one's personality, usually the "dark side," that their consciousness tries to deny. The less someone consciously acknowledges their shadow self, thought Jung, the "blacker and denser it is." The demon inside that we have tried to banish, exile, murder, still rises to the surface, anyway.

We try to compensate for this dark side by bringing in light, but all that does is try to balance it. It does not actually make the darkness go away.

I wonder: is there ever enough light to make darkness go away? Once you have evil inside you, is there any level of divinity that can abolish your sins?

It's what my dad was trying to work out, I think. He didn't join the board of the child abuse foundation to cover up or hide who he "really" was; he did it to try to balance out this dark side of himself. A side he very much wanted to pretend never existed — not just because he knew it was legally or morally wrong. He wanted to pretend it never existed because he didn't want to be a bad man. He wanted, he tried, to get away from the bad men who haunted his childhood: the alcoholics, the abusers, the men who withheld love.

50   My dad did not want to be the kind of man who would molest his son.

Steve was more important to my dad than anyone or anything on this earth — certainly more than me. When my brother suffered, my dad suffered. The part of my dad that hurt Steve was dark and shadowy and probably caused my dad nearly as much pain as it caused Steve. I believe he would have abolished it, if he could.

I am sure that most of the time, my dad lived in the land of good and light. He built a play kitchen in the basement for his daughter and a wood Kool-Aid stand for his son, he taught us both to play softball and baseball, he went to all of Steve's games and for one season volunteered as an umpire at my softball games. He believed in God and studied Jung and wrote poetry about the soul. This is the man my father wanted to be and he got so, so close. But there was never enough light to abolish his darkness. Pedophilia, frotteurism, debase, pervert, invalidate, rape.

My dad was not a monster. He had a monster inside, and although there is probably little difference to his victims, it's made a difference to me. I don't condone what he did, but I do feel the one thing I sense you're never supposed to feel for a sexual violator: compassion. Compassion that his childhood occurred in such dark loss and that he tried so hard to escape, but, no matter what, was never able to get away. It would always be inside him. I have either the benefit or the burden—depending on how you look at it—of loving my dad. And even though I assumed this newfound information should have made me un-love him, it doesn't work that way. Not for me, at least. For me, the way it works is that I try to understand. I will never know exactly what and when, but maybe I can form a glimpse into how and why. It would be different if he were still alive—I know that—and not because I could demand the truth from him. He would not tell the truth, he would deny, and that denial would make me hate him as much as the acts themselves. This way, I get to work it through my own framework, which is, of course, distorted and subjective in its own particular way.

I wish I could talk to the women he raped and give them something. What? Would a hug from me somehow make better this decades-old violation? Of course not. But I want to look them in the eyes and say, "I know what he did and it was not okay." If my brother was still alive, I would not say these words to him out loud. But I would hold his hand and stroke his head and telegraph silently, *You sweet, innocent boy. You deserved so much more.*

Something else I brought home from my dad's house, after both he and Steve died: their ashes. My dad's in an Asian-decorated urn, my brother's in a heavy green cardboard box. For years, they have sat in my garage. I assumed that one day I would take them to Maui, to the place we used to vacation, and I would sprinkle their ashes together, into the ocean, so they could remain bound forever.

Now I know I can't do that to Steve. I hope his death has allowed him to finally be free of our dad and all the chains that entailed. I will not, even symbolically, shackle him to our dad again. I will take my brother's ashes to Hawaii one day and scatter them at sea or into an ancient volcano, and maybe by making him more disperse, I will somehow make him whole.

My dad's ashes remain a conundrum. I thought of sending them back to Aguilar, to the cemetery where his mother and father and sister and all those other doomed family members are buried. But then I'd be banishing him to what he tried so hard to get away from. Even though I live with the knowledge that he did not ever completely escape the darkness of his family, it feels cruel to resign him to this destiny.

I realize these are just ashes. They are not actually my dad or brother's soul or self, neither their dark side or light side, just remnants of their corporeal being. Where I scatter their ashes will not change my dad or brother's destiny. But, maybe, it will change mine.

Statement on the National Industrial Recovery Act

Franklin Delano Roosevelt

Franklin Delano Roosevelt (1882–1945) was the thirty-second President of the United States, from 1933 until his death twelve years later. Roosevelt's presidency spanned most of the Great Depression and World War II. Roosevelt contracted polio in 1921, but he went on to become a member of the New York State Senate, Secretary of the Navy, and Governor of New York before being elected president. At the outset of his presidency, Roosevelt spearheaded the New Deal—a series of federal programs designed to help the US out of the Depression. One of those programs, the National Industrial Recovery Act of 1933, was designed to jump-start the economy.

The law I have just signed was passed to put people back to work, to let them buy more of the products of farms and factories and start our business at a living rate again. This task is in two stages; first, to get many hundreds of thousands of the unemployed back on the payroll by snowfall and, second, to plan for a better future for the longer pull. While we shall not neglect the second, the first stage is an emergency job. It has the right of way.

The second part of the Act gives employment through a vast program of public works. Our studies show that we should be able to hire many men at once and to step up to about a million new jobs by October 1st, and a much greater number later. We must put at the head of our list those works which are fully ready to start now. Our first purpose is to create employment as fast as we can, but we should not pour money into unproved projects.

We have worked out our plans for action. Some of the work will start tomorrow. I am making available $400,000,000 for State roads under regulations which I have just signed, and I am told that the States will get this work under way at once. I have also just released over $200,000,000 for the Navy to start building ships under the London Treaty.

In my Inaugural I laid down the simple proposition that nobody is going to starve in this country. It seems to me to be equally plain that no business which depends for existence on paying less than living wages to its workers has any right to continue in this country. By "business" I mean the whole of commerce as well as the whole of industry; by workers I mean all workers, the white collar class as well as the men in overalls; and by living wages I mean more than a bare subsistence level—I mean the wages of decent living.

5 Throughout industry, the change from starvation wages and starvation employment to living wages and sustained employment can, in large part, be made by an industrial covenant to which all employers shall subscribe. It is greatly to their interest to do this because decent living, widely spread among our 125,000,000 people, eventually means the opening up to industry of the richest market which the world has known. It is the only way to utilize the so-called excess capacity of our industrial plants. This is the principle that makes this one of the most important laws that ever has come from Congress because, before the passage of this Act, no such industrial covenant was possible.

On this idea, the first part of the Act proposes to our industry a great spontaneous cooperation to put millions of men back in their regular jobs this summer. The idea is simply for employers to hire more men to do the existing work by reducing the work-hours of each man's week and at the same time paying a living wage for the shorter week.

No employer and no group of less than all employers in a single trade could do this alone and continue to live in business competition. But if all employers in each trade now band themselves faithfully in these modern guilds—without exception-and agree to act together and at once, none will be hurt and millions of workers, so long deprived of the right to earn their bread in the sweat of their labor, can raise their heads again. The challenge of this law is whether we can sink selfish interest and present a solid front against a common peril.

It is a challenge to industry which has long insisted that, given the right to act in unison, it could do much for the general good which has hitherto been unlawful. From today it has that right.

Many good men voted this new charter with misgivings. I do not share these doubts. I had part in the great cooperation of 1917 and 1918 and it is my faith that we can count on our industry once more to join in our general purpose to lift this new threat and to do it without taking any advantage of the public trust which has this day been reposed without stint in the good faith and high purpose of American business.

But industry is challenged in another way. It is not only the slackers within trade groups who may stand in the path of our common purpose. In a sense these groups compete with each other, and no single industry, and no separate cluster of industries, can do this job alone for exactly the same reason that no single employer can do it alone. In other words, we can imagine such a thing as a slacker industry.

This law is also a challenge to labor. Workers, too, are here given a new charter of rights long sought and hitherto denied. But they know that the first move expected by the Nation is a great cooperation of all employers, by one single mass-action, to improve the case of workers on a scale never attempted in any Nation. Industries can do this only if they have the support of the whole public and especially of their own workers. This is not a law to foment discord and it will not be executed as such. This is a time for mutual confidence and help and we can safely rely on the sense of fair play among all Americans to assure every industry which now moves forward promptly in this united drive against depression that its workers will be with it to a man.

It is, further, a challenge to administration. We are relaxing some of the safeguards of the anti-trust laws. The public must be protected against the abuses that led to their enactment, and to this end, we are putting in place of old principles of unchecked competition some new Government controls. They must, above all, be impartial and just. Their purpose is to free business, not to shackle it; and no man who stands on the constructive, forward-looking side of his industry has anything to fear from them. To such men the opportunities for individual initiative will open more amply than ever. Let me make it clear, however, that the anti-trust laws still stand firmly against monopolies that restrain trade and price fixing which allows inordinate profits or unfairly high prices.

If we ask our trade groups to do that which exposes their business, as never before, to undermining by members who are unwilling to do their part, we must guard those who play the game for the general good against those who may seek selfish gains from the unselfishness of others. We must protect them from the racketeers who invade organizations of both employers and workers. We are spending billions of dollars and if that spending is really to serve our ends, it must be done quickly. We must see that our haste does not permit favoritism and graft. All this is a heavy load for any Government and one that can be borne only if we have the patience, cooperation, and support of people everywhere.

Finally, this law is a challenge to our whole people. There is no power in America that can force against the public will such action as we require. But there is no group in America that can withstand the force of an aroused public opinion. This great cooperation can succeed only if those who bravely go forward to restore jobs have aggressive public support and those who lag are made to feel the full weight of public disapproval.

As to the machinery, we shall use the practical way of accomplish- 15
ing what we are setting out to do. When a trade association has a code ready to submit and the association has qualified as truly representative, and after reasonable notice has been issued to all concerned, a public hearing will be held by the Administrator or a deputy. A Labor Advisory Board appointed by the Secretary of Labor will be responsible that every affected labor group, whether organized or unorganized, is fully and adequately represented in an advisory capacity and any interested labor group will be entitled to be heard through representatives of its own choosing. An Industrial Advisory Board appointed by the Secretary of Commerce will be responsible that every affected industrial group is fully and adequately represented in an advisory capacity and any interested industrial group will be entitled to be heard through representatives of its own choosing. A Consumers Advisory Board will be responsible that the interests of the consuming public will be represented and every reasonable opportunity will be given to any group or class who may be affected directly or indirectly to present their views.

At the conclusion of these hearings and after the most careful scrutiny by a competent economic staff, the Administrator will present the subject to me for my action under the law.

I am fully aware that wage increases will eventually raise costs, but I ask that managements give first consideration to the improvement of operating figures by greatly increased sales to be expected from the rising purchasing power of the public. That is good economics and good business. The aim of this whole effort is to restore our rich domestic market by raising its vast consuming capacity. If we now inflate prices as fast and as far as we increase wages, the whole project will be set at naught. We cannot hope for the full effect of this plan unless, in these first critical months, and, even at the expense of full initial profits, we defer price increases as long as possible. If we can thus start a strong, sound, upward spiral of business activity, our industries will have little doubt of black-ink operations in the last quarter of this year. The pent-up demand of this people is very great and if we can release it on so broad a front, we need not fear a lagging recovery. There is greater danger of too much feverish speed.

In a few industries, there has been some forward buying at unduly depressed prices in recent weeks. Increased costs resulting from this Government-inspired movement may make it very hard for some manufacturers and jobbers to fulfill some of their present contracts without loss. It will be a part of this wide industrial cooperation for those having the benefit of these forward bargains (contracted before the law was passed) to take the initiative in revising them to absorb some share of the increase in their suppliers' costs, thus raised in the public interest. It is only in such a willing and considerate spirit, throughout the whole of industry, that we can hope to succeed.

Under Title I of this Act, I have appointed Hugh Johnson as Administrator and a special Industrial Recovery Board under the Chairmanship of the Secretary of Commerce. This organization is now prepared to receive proposed Codes and to conduct prompt hearings looking toward their submission to me for approval. While acceptable proposals of no trade group will be delayed, it is my hope that the ten major industries which control the bulk of industrial employment can submit their simple basic Codes at once and that the country can look forward to the month of July as the beginning of our great national movement back to work.

During the coming three weeks, Title II relating to public works   20 and construction projects will be temporarily conducted by Colonel Donald H. Sawyer as administrator and a special temporary board consisting of the Secretary of the Interior as Chairman, the Secretary of Commerce, the Secretary of Agriculture, the Secretary of War, the Attorney General, the Secretary of Labor and the Director of the Budget.

During the next two weeks, the Administrator and this board will make a study of all projects already submitted or to be submitted and, as previously stated, certain allotments under the new law will be made immediately.

Between these twin efforts—public works and industrial re-employment—it is not too much to expect that a great many men and women can be taken from the ranks of the unemployed before winter comes. It is the most important attempt of this kind in history. As in the great crisis of the World War, it puts a whole people to the simple but vital test—"Must we go on in many groping, disorganized, separate units to defeat or shall we move as one great team to victory?"

Impressions of the East Side

Margaret H. Sanger

Margaret Sanger (1879–1966) opened the first birth control clinic in the United States, in 1916, after which she was arrested for handing out pamphlets on family planning. That was not her first clash with the law on that subject, nor was it her last. Sanger is considered a pioneer of the reproductive rights movement, promoting the idea that women needed to be able to decide when and whether to have children, in order to achieve social equality. She is a generally admired but controversial figure. Her work as a nurse in the slums of New York City informs her perspective in this essay.

Part I

When you walk through the streets of the much talked about East Side you come away with the feeling that you have seen all of it you wish to see. When you pass through Cherry street and emerge from its depths with fish scales and fruit stains on your clothing, you feel quite satisfied with the glimpse you have had of it, and with both hands up exclaim "Never again!"

But the East Side thus seen from the outside is nothing compared to the living hell within its walls. To eat with its people, to sleep with them, to buy where they buy, to listen to their quarrels, gossip, tales of sorrow, sickness and fears, is to see them as they are in their daily life.

Everything is thrown out of the windows; garbage is rolled up in newspapers and thrown into the courts, when there is one; if not, then into the streets. A piece of meat is eaten and the bone thrown out of the window; so are dead rats, dead cats, decayed vegetables. And in cases where the toilets are in use by the many families on the same

238

floor, the mother allows the children to use paper as toilet receptacles, and that, too, is thrown out of the window.

In very clean places the courts are cleaned once a month, but where the windows overlook so-called sheds, these are cleaned only when conditions become so vile that the tenants threaten to leave.

Everybody complains of this filthy habit of throwing things out   5 of the windows, and everyone denies having any part in doing it!

Then the vermin. In one of the small flats, the kitchen was swarming with, not thousands, but millions of roaches. They were piled four layers high in places and in corners they were stacked up several inches high. Cobwebs hung from the ceiling, and touched your head as you entered. Bed bugs, too, are everywhere, and on the hot nights the moaning and crying of the little children show how their sleep is disturbed by the vermin. It is pitiful to hear the cries of often ten or more children all at once as the houses are so near; it of course keeps every one nearby awake, and shouts of "Shut up" issue forth from the men who must get their night's rest in order to keep their jobs.

After the poverty and filth, the next thing which leaves its lasting impression on you is the ignorant cruelty with which the people of the East Side treat their children. Everybody strikes the children, parents, neighbors, sisters, boarders; in fact, everyone seems to take a slap at the children, for any trifling thing, and yet every parent thinks himself a model parent. It is most common to see a father strike his 6 or 8-year-old boy with the same force he would strike at a man. "I'll smash you," he says, but fortunately the little fellow has learned how to dodge.

Thousands of mothers leave their little children in the care of the older boy or girl (usually not over 9 years old) and go to work early in the morning in the factories or work shops to return at night to do the work of the family. First the mother does the washing which takes until 2 in the morning; the next night she irons, which takes the same time, and so on with the scrubbing, cleaning, and mending. Then it is time to do the washing again, and so on, in this terrible existence, day after day this worn out and half-famished mother continues her burden of life. The woman who does not do this work at night, being too tired or half sick, is considered "lazy" by the neighbors, and all her misfortune is summed up in her "laziness."

With the food that one gets at even the "rich" families, it is difficult to continue work until noon without stocking up again, so little do they understand combinations of food or the requirements of the human system. It is a common sight, too, to see a workingman, working on the streets, stop at the noon hour and with the hunk of bread which he brought with him, go to a nearby stand and buy a penny's worth of watermelon.

10   Some of the mothers close the house all day, and give the children bread and tea to stay in the parks until night time. Others give over the responsibility to the oldest child and let them run in and out as they choose, with no guidance, no care or instruction. Is it not marvelous that they continue meek and docile?

One of the greatest blessings of the East Side came when the milk stations were instituted. The milk is prepared at the stations by trained nurses, for special ages, and it is increased according to age. Should the child not thrive and the parent think it is not doing well, the mother takes it to the station where it is examined by physicians, and either barley water or a different preparation is given for the child, all without extra cost. They give nine bottles with two and a half ounces of milk for an infant (and that is all they can have), at 1 cent a bottle. Later on, when the quantity of milk is increased, the charges are a little more, but the fact that the bottles are washed, sterilized, and sealed by trained hands almost insures the life of the child against disease. The infant at least has the proper food, for even when the mother is in the factory the children go for the milk, give the name of the child and receive the milk and give it to the baby during the day. Every individual child is registered and has its special milk.

Again, one of the terrible sights which meets your gaze is the army of little pale-faced children which come into the streets at night to play. Accustomed to seeing the children, although ragged and filthy at least browned by the sun, playing about in the day time, your attention is attracted to these white and drawn faces and you inquire about them. You are told that these little children, anywhere around 10 years of age, are products of the sweatshops. There they work all day, sometimes in cellars, picking over old rags, and sometimes in "shops" carrying huge bundles from place to place.

The very thought is nauseous, that where there are thousands of able-bodied men willing and glad to work, these little pale-faced girls with shoulders already bent, should spend their childhood days struggling for an existence. The parents of these little ones are loathe to send them to work, but each added baby makes it harder for them to fight off starvation, and anything which offers relief from worry and debt is acceptable to even the most loving parents. And as they watch these little toilers join hands with the other children and sing "Sweet Land of Liberty" the hope springs up in their breasts that perhaps some "luck" will come to them, and the children will be able to go to school again.

The younger generation of women are no more anxious than their uptown sisters to have large families, and these young women are easy victims for the many fake and quack physicians who inhabit the East Side. One woman aged 72, said she would gladly have another baby if nature were willing, but her daughters and sons, who had endured poverty and neglect, remembering what a nightmare their childhood had been, preferred risking imprisonment and death, rather than bearing children and have them go through what they lived through.

Part II

15   The East Side is full of superstition. Superstitious fear prompts them in many of their acts. If they can give a penny to a blind man, they feel sure it will bring them "luck;" they fear to mix meat and milk, not so much because of religious scruples as because it brings them bad "luck." One of the desires of their life is to move up town, to cleaner quarters, but even when they are able to, the fear that "luck" will leave them, keeps them down town. A physician of some repute, living down town, when asked why he lives down there when his practice is mostly up town, said, "'Luck' came to him there and he will stay with it." Almost everything depends on "luck," to them it seems almost a part of their religion, and is difficult to overcome.

Their great desire is to get "rich" and employ men and women. The capitalistic instinct to be your own "boss" and make off the labor of others is everywhere. It is ridiculous to think for a moment that the class struggle is on the East Side only and every one who understands the meaning of the words, knows only too well that it is everywhere. But certainly it is at its height on the East Side, for there it is the aim and ambition of everybody to bleed everybody else. The doctors, druggists and lawyers all take a share in this. The druggists charge from 10 to 15 cents more on every article than is paid elsewhere.

An example of the doctor's bleeding is shown by the story which follows: During the very hot weather a rash broke out on an infant whose parents had had a little "luck" in accumulating this world's goods. The ever kind neighbors and friends of the parents advised them to go to a baby specialist, just for a change of "luck," they said, as the baby had not been well since birth. These were easily persuaded, and the first visit cost them $5. The specialist then sent the mother to another physician to have her milk tested, which cost five more. Then both parents had to have their blood tested, which cost five each, and go back again to the first specialist to tell him there was nothing the matter with either the milk or the blood, which cost five more, or $25 in all. And the first day it grew a little cooler the baby's rash disappeared!

It is surprising to see the large number of push carts, and one wonders how they can exist there, when it is impossible for some people to buy only the bare necessities of life. But the fact is that over half of the people there do not patronize the push carts, and the other half who do are compelled to buy the same articles over and over again, so cheap are the wares. A pair of stockings cost 15 cents, but after one day's moderate wear they are unfit for darning, so badly and of such wretched material are they made.

The fruit peddlers too astonish you at the thriving business they seem to do. But when you have eaten with these people for a few days the same erratic appetite takes hold of you, and meat, fish and bread no longer satisfy you, and if there is a cent to be had you find yourself on your way to the fruit carts too, eagerly longing to quench the terrible hunger which has taken possession of you. The people are always eating, for they are always hungry.

The parents' love of the little ones is almost animal like in its emotions, especially to those under four, after that — well — it's just like waiting for the years to pass till they can bring in some return for their earthly existence.

The shouting, screaming and swearing at the children and even at the infants, is impossible to conceive of, having had no childhood themselves it is difficult for them to realize the evolution or state of the child mind, and a child of four or five is expected to think and act like the parents, which accounts for the many slaps the little tots get all around. They are proud to call their children Americans, and when they are able, or brave enough to try their "luck," in a new section, they emerge to the upper East Side. There they rapidly develop, and improve in manners, language and habits. In a few years they have outgrown that neighborhood and the West Side becomes their Mecca.

The word Socialism is almost a household word among them. They have neither the fear, nor have they the disgust which our friends up town have of the word. Yet the deep, and abject pity with which they regard you when they discover that you are a Socialist is a hundred times more maddening and much more difficult to meet. If you had escaped from an asylum with a placard of "harmless" on you they could not treat you with more tenderness. They will even listen to you while you expound your Socialism to them, but when you have finished they will smilingly shake their heads, and tell you that it is a beautiful dream, but as long as the world lasts, "Brains" will be the only thing that can count. On their explaining just what "Brains" mean, you find that the principle the druggist used when he charged them 10 cents more than the article could be purchased for elsewhere is the brilliant example.

A Latina Judge's Voice

Sonia Sotomayor

Sonia Sotomayor (b. 1954) has served as an Associate Justice of the Supreme Court of the United States since 2009. She is the first Hispanic person and the third woman to serve on the Court. Her parents were born in Puerto Rico; Sotomayor grew up in the Bronx in New York City and identifies as "Nuyorican." She graduated from Princeton University and Yale Law School. During her Supreme Court confirmation hearings, much was made of a remark from a 2001 speech that Sotomayor made at the University of California, Berkeley, School of Law, in which she posited that a "wise Latina" could perhaps make better judgements than a white man. This is an excerpt of that speech.

October 26, 2001 — UC Berkeley School of Law
Judge Mario G. Olmos Memorial Lecture

I intend tonight to touch upon the themes that this conference will be discussing this weekend and to talk to you about my Latina identity, where it came from, and the influence I perceive it has on my presence on the bench.

Who am I? I am a "Newyorkrican." For those of you on the West Coast who do not know what that term means: I am a born and bred New Yorker of Puerto Rican-born parents who came to the states during World War II.

Like many other immigrants to this great land, my parents came 5
because of poverty and to attempt to find and secure a better life for themselves and the family that they hoped to have. They largely succeeded. For that, my brother and I are very grateful. The story of that success is what made me and what makes me the Latina that I am.

The Latina side of my identity was forged and closely nurtured by my family through our shared experiences and traditions.

For me, a very special part of my being Latina is the mucho platos de arroz, gandoles y pernir — rice, beans and pork — that I have eaten at countless family holidays and special events. My Latina identity also includes, because of my particularly adventurous taste buds, morcilla — pig intestines, patitas de cerdo con garbanzo — pigs' feet with beans, and la lengua y orejas de cuchifrito, pigs' tongue and ears. I bet the Mexican-Americans in this room are thinking that Puerto Ricans have unusual food tastes. Some of us, like me, do. Part of my Latina identity is the sound of merengue at all our family parties and the heart wrenching Spanish love songs that we enjoy. It is the memory of Saturday afternoon at the movies with my aunt and cousins watching Cantinflas, who is not Puerto Rican, but who was an icon Spanish comedian on par with Abbot and Costello of my generation. My Latina soul was nourished as I visited and played at my grandmother's house with my cousins and extended family. They were my friends as I grew up. Being a Latina child was watching the adults playing dominos on Saturday night and us kids playing lotería, bingo, with my grandmother calling out the numbers which we marked on our cards with chick peas.

Now, does any one of these things make me a Latina? Obviously not because each of our Caribbean and Latin American communities has their own unique food and different traditions at the holidays. I only learned about tacos in college from my Mexican-American roommate. Being a Latina in America also does not mean speaking Spanish. I happen to speak it fairly well. But my brother, only three years younger, like too many of us educated here, barely speaks it. Most of us born and bred here, speak it very poorly. . . .

America has a deeply confused image of itself that is in perpetual tension. We are a nation that takes pride in our ethnic diversity, recognizing its importance in shaping our society and in adding richness to its existence. Yet, we simultaneously insist that we can and must function and live in a race and color-blind way that ignore these very differences that in other contexts we laud. That tension between "the melting pot and the salad bowl"—a recently popular metaphor used to described New York's diversity—is being hotly debated today in national discussions about affirmative action. Many of us struggle with this tension and attempt to maintain and promote our cultural and ethnic identities in a society that is often ambivalent about how to deal with its differences. In this time of great debate we must remember that it is not political struggles that create a Latino or Latina identity. I became a Latina by the way I love and the way I live my life. My family showed me by their example how wonderful and vibrant life is and how wonderful and magical it is to have a Latina soul. They taught me to love being a Puerto Riqueña and to love America and value its lesson that great things could be achieved if one works hard for it. But achieving success here is no easy accomplishment for Latinos or Latinas, and although that struggle did not and does not create a Latina identity, it does inspire how I live my life. . . .

Whether born from experience or inherent physiological or cultural differences . . . our gender and national origins may and will make a difference in our judging. Justice [Sandra Day] O'Connor has often been cited as saying that a wise old man and wise old woman will reach the same conclusion in deciding cases. I am not so sure Justice O'Connor is the author of that line since Professor [Judith] Resnik attributes that line to [New York State] Supreme Court Justice [Hugh] Coyle. I am also not so sure that I agree with the statement. First, as Professor Martha Minnow has noted, there can never be a universal definition of wise. Second, I would hope that a wise Latina woman with the richness of her experiences would more often than not reach a better conclusion than a white male who hasn't lived that life.

10   Let us not forget that wise men like [Supreme Court Justice] Oliver Wendell Holmes and Justice [Benjamin] Cardozo voted on cases which upheld both sex and race discrimination in our society. Until 1972, no Supreme Court case ever upheld the claim of a woman in a gender discrimination case. I . . . believe that we should not be so myopic as to believe that others of different experiences or backgrounds are incapable of understanding the values and needs of people from a different group. Many are so capable. As [United States District] Judge [Miriam Goldman] Cedarbaum pointed out to me, nine white men on the Supreme Court in the past have done so on many occasions and on many issues including Brown [v. Board of Education].

However, to understand takes time and effort, something that not all people are willing to give. For others, their experiences limit their ability to understand the experiences of others. Others simply do not care. Hence, one must accept the proposition that a difference there will be by the presence of women and people of color on the bench. Personal experiences affect the facts that judges choose to see. My hope is that I will take the good from my experiences and extrapolate them further into areas with which I am unfamiliar. I simply do not know exactly what that difference will be in my judging. But I accept there will be some based on my gender and my Latina heritage.

I also hope that by raising the question today of what difference having more Latinos and Latinas on the bench will make will start your own evaluation. For people of color and women lawyers, what does and should being an ethnic minority mean in your lawyering? For men lawyers, what areas in your experiences and attitudes do you need to work on to make you capable of reaching those great moments of enlightenment which other men in different circumstances have been able to reach. For all of us, how do we change the facts that in every task force study of gender and race bias in the courts, women and people of color, lawyers and judges alike, report in significantly higher percentages than white men that their gender and race has shaped their careers, from hiring, retention to promotion and that a statistically significant number of women and minority lawyers and judges, both alike, have experienced bias in the courtroom?

Each day on the bench I learn something new about the judicial process and about being a professional Latina woman in a world that sometimes looks at me with suspicion. I am reminded each day that I render decisions that affect people concretely and that I owe them constant and complete vigilance in checking my assumptions, presumptions and perspectives and ensuring that to the extent that my limited abilities and capabilities permit me, that I reevaluate them and change as circumstances and cases before me requires. I can and do aspire to be greater than the sum total of my experiences but I accept my limitations. I willingly accept that we who judge must not deny the differences resulting from experience and heritage but attempt, as the Supreme Court suggests, continuously to judge when those opinions, sympathies and prejudices are appropriate.

There is always a danger embedded in relative morality, but since judging is a series of choices that we must make, that I am forced to make, I hope that I can make them by informing myself on the questions I must not avoid asking and continuously pondering. We, I mean all of us in this room, must continue individually and in voices united in organizations that have supported this conference, to think about these questions and to figure out how we go about creating the opportunity for there to be more women and people of color on the bench so we can finally have statistically significant numbers to measure the differences we will and are making. . . .

Standing Up for Our Law Enforcement Community

In 2017, the White House published a statement on its website on the role of law enforcement in the United States under President Donald Trump. The statement highlights Trump's common talking points about safety from crime, a border wall, and protecting the Second Amendment.

One of the fundamental rights of every American is to live in a safe community. A Trump Administration will empower our law enforcement officers to do their jobs and keep our streets free of crime and violence. The Trump Administration will be a law and order administration. President Trump will honor our men and women in uniform and will support their mission of protecting the public. The dangerous anti-police atmosphere in America is wrong. The Trump Administration will end it.

The Trump Administration is committed to reducing violent crime. In 2015, homicides increased by 17% in America's fifty largest cities. That's the largest increase in 25 years. In our nation's capital, killings rose by 50 percent over the past four years. There were thousands of shootings in Chicago last year alone.

Our country needs more law enforcement, more community engagement, and more effective policing.

Our job is not to make life more comfortable for the rioter, the looter, or the violent disrupter. Our job is to make life more comfortable for parents who want their kids to be able to walk the streets safely. Or the senior citizen waiting for a bus. Or the young child walking home from school.

Supporting law enforcement means supporting our citizens' abil- 5
ity to protect themselves. We will uphold Americans' Second Amendment rights at every level of our judicial system.

President Trump is committed to building a border wall to stop
illegal immigration, to stop the gangs and the violence, and to stop
the drugs from pouring into our communities. He is dedicated to
enforcing our border laws, ending sanctuary cities, and stemming the
tide of lawlessness associated with illegal immigration.

Supporting law enforcement also means deporting illegal aliens
with violent criminal records who have remained within our borders.

It is the first duty of government to keep the innocent safe, and
President Donald Trump will fight for the safety of every American,
and especially those Americans who have not known safe neighborhoods for a very long time.

Ain't I a Woman?

Sojourner Truth

Isabella Baumfree (c.1797–1883) was born into slavery in Ulster County, New York. She was an abolitionist, author, and human rights activist, and she was the first black woman to win back her enslaved child from a white man in court. Her most famous speech, "Ain't I a Woman?," was delivered without preparation at the Ohio Women's Rights Convention in 1851. Different transcriptions of the speech exist, often in Southern dialect, which seems unlikely, since Truth spoke only Dutch until she was nine years old.

Well, children, where there is so much racket, there must be something out of kilter. I think that between the niggers of the South and the women at the North, all talking about rights, the white men will be in a fix pretty soon. But what's all this here talking about?

That man over there say that women needs to be helped into carriages, lifted over ditches, and to have the best place everywhere. Nobody ever helps me into carriages, or over mud-puddles, or gives me any best place! And ain't I a woman?

Look at me! Look at my arm! I have ploughed, and planted, and gathered into barns, and no man could head me! And ain't I a woman? I could work as much and eat as much as a man when I could get it—and bear the lash as well! And ain't I a woman? And when I cried out with my mother's grief, none but Jesus heard me. And ain't I a woman?

Then they talk about this thing in the head; what's this they call it? ["Intellect" someone whispers near.] That's right, honey. What's that got to do with women's rights or niggers' rights? If my cup won't hold but a pint, and yours holds a quart, wouldn't you be mean not to let me have my little half-measure full?

Then that little man in black there, he says women can't have as 5 much rights as men, because Christ wasn't a woman! Where did your Christ come from? Where did your Christ come from? From God and a woman! Men had nothing to do with Him.

If the first woman God ever made was strong enough to turn the world upside down all alone, these women together ought to be able to turn it back, and get it right side up again! And now that they are asking to do it, the men better let them! Obliged to you for hearing me, and now old Sojourner has got nothing more to say.

Worried Man Blues

"Worried Man Blues" is a traditional folk song passed down by oral tradition, which may have originated as early as the late 19th century. Recorded versions date back to 1930. The lyrics follow the standard blues convention of a repeated first line.

It takes a worried man to sing a worried song.
It takes a worried man to sing a worried song.
It takes a worried man to sing a worried song.
I'm worried now, but I won't be worried long.

I went across the river, and I lay down to sleep.
I went across the river, and I lay down to sleep.
I went across the river, and I lay down to sleep.
When I woke up, I had shackles on my feet.

The shackles on my feet had 21 links of chain.
. . . .
And on each link, the initials of my name.

I asked that judge, "Tell me what's gonna be my fine?"
. . . .
"21 years on the Rocky Mountain line!"

The train came to the station, 21 coaches long.
. . . .
The one I love is on that train and gone.

I looked down the track as far as I could see
. . . .

A little bitty hand was waving after me.

If anyone should ask you who made up this song,
. . . .
Tell 'em 'twas I, and I sing it all day long.

It takes a worried man to sing a worried song.
It takes a worried man to sing a worried song.
It takes a worried man to sing a worried song.
I'm worried now, but I won't be worried long.

The School Days of an Indian Girl

Zitkala-Sa

Zitkala-Sa (1876–1938) was born on the Yankton Indian Reservation in South Dakota. At eight years old, she was taken by missionaries to White's Manual Labor Institute, a boarding school in Indiana, and given the name Gertrude Simmons. She was the author of the first Native American opera, as well as collections of Native American legends, political writings, and articles. From 1918 to 1919, she edited American Indian Magazine, *a publication of the Society of American Indians. The following is from her 1921 collection,* American Indian Stories.

I. The Land of Red Apples

There were eight in our party of bronzed children who were going East with the missionaries. Among us were three young braves, two tall girls, and we three little ones, Judéwin, Thowin, and I.

We had been very impatient to start on our journey to the Red Apple Country, which, we were told, lay a little beyond the great circular horizon of the Western prairie. Under a sky of rosy apples we dreamt of roaming as freely and happily as we had chased the cloud shadows on the Dakota plains. We had anticipated much pleasure from a ride on the iron horse, but the throngs of staring palefaces disturbed and troubled us.

On the train, fair women, with tottering babies on each arm, stopped their haste and scrutinized the children of absent mothers. Large men, with heavy bundles in their hands, halted nearby, and riveted their glassy blue eyes upon us.

I sank deep into the corner of my seat, for I resented being watched. Directly in front of me, children who were no larger than I hung themselves upon the backs of their seats, with their bold white faces toward me. Sometimes they took their forefingers out of their mouths and pointed at my moccasined feet. Their mothers, instead of reproving such rude curiosity, looked closely at me, and attracted their children's further notice to my blanket. This embarrassed me, and kept me constantly on the verge of tears.

I sat perfectly still, with my eyes downcast, daring only now and   5
then to shoot long glances around me. Chancing to turn to the window at my side, I was quite breathless upon seeing one familiar object. It was the telegraph pole which strode by at short paces. Very near my mother's dwelling, along the edge of a road thickly bordered with wild sunflowers, some poles like these had been planted by white men. Often I had stopped, on my way down the road, to hold my ear against the pole, and, hearing its low moaning, I used to wonder what the paleface had done to hurt it. Now I sat watching for each pole that glided by to be the last one.

In this way I had forgotten my uncomfortable surroundings, when I heard one of my comrades call out my name. I saw the missionary standing very near, tossing candies and gums into our midst. This amused us all, and we tried to see who could catch the most of the sweetmeats.

Though we rode several days inside of the iron horse, I do not recall a single thing about our luncheons.

It was night when we reached the school grounds. The lights from the windows of the large buildings fell upon some of the icicled trees that stood beneath them. We were led toward an open door, where the brightness of the lights within flooded out over the heads of the excited palefaces who blocked the way. My body trembled more from fear than from the snow I trod upon.

Entering the house, I stood close against the wall. The strong glaring light in the large whitewashed room dazzled my eyes. The noisy hurrying of hard shoes upon a bare wooden floor increased the whirring in my ears. My only safety seemed to be in keeping next to the wall. As I was wondering in which direction to escape from all this confusion, two warm hands grasped me firmly, and in the same moment I was tossed high in midair. A rosy-cheeked paleface woman caught me in her arms. I was both frightened and insulted by such trifling. I stared into her eyes, wishing her to let me stand on my own feet, but she jumped me up and down with increasing enthusiasm. My mother had never made a plaything of her wee daughter. Remembering this, I began to cry aloud.

10   They misunderstood the cause of my tears, and placed me at a white table loaded with food. There our party were united again. As I did not hush my crying, one of the older ones whispered to me, "Wait until you are alone in the night."

It was very little I could swallow besides my sobs, that evening.

"Oh, I want my mother and my brother Dawée! I want to go to my aunt!" I pleaded; but the ears of the palefaces could not hear me.

From the table we were taken along an upward incline of wooden boxes, which I learned afterward to call a stairway. At the top was a quiet hall, dimly lighted. Many narrow beds were in one straight line down the entire length of the wall. In them lay sleeping brown faces, which peeped just out of the coverings. I was tucked into bed with one of the tall girls, because she talked to me in my mother tongue and seemed to soothe me.

I had arrived in the wonderful land of rosy skies, but I was not happy, as I had thought I should be. My long travel and the bewildering sights had exhausted me. I fell asleep, heaving deep, tired sobs. My tears were left to dry themselves in streaks, because neither my aunt nor my mother was near to wipe them away.

II. The Cutting Of My Long Hair

The first day in the land of apples was a bitter-cold one; for the snow 15
still covered the ground, and the trees were bare. A large bell rang for
breakfast, its loud metallic voice crashing through the belfry overhead
and into our sensitive ears. The annoying clatter of shoes on bare
floors gave us no peace. The constant clash of harsh noises, with an
undercurrent of many voices murmuring an unknown tongue, made
a bedlam within which I was securely tied. And though my spirit tore
itself in struggling for its lost freedom, all was useless.

A paleface woman, with white hair, came up after us. We were
placed in a line of girls who were marching into the dining room.
These were Indian girls, in stiff shoes and closely clinging dresses. The
small girls wore sleeved aprons and shingled hair. As I walked noise-
lessly in my soft moccasins, I felt like sinking to the floor, for my blanket had been stripped from my shoulders. I looked hard at the Indian
girls, who seemed not to care that they were even more immodestly
dressed than I, in their tightly fitting clothes. While we marched in,
the boys entered at an opposite door. I watched for the three young
braves who came in our party. I spied them in the rear ranks, looking
as uncomfortable as I felt.

A small bell was tapped, and each of the pupils drew a chair from
under the table. Supposing this act meant they were to be seated, I
pulled out mine and at once slipped into it from one side. But when I
turned my head, I saw that I was the only one seated, and all the rest
at our table remained standing. Just as I began to rise, looking shyly
around to see how chairs were to be used, a second bell was sounded.
All were seated at last, and I had to crawl back into my chair again. I
heard a man's voice at one end of the hall, and I looked around to see

him. But all the others hung their heads over their plates. As I glanced at the long chain of tables, I caught the eyes of a paleface woman upon me. Immediately I dropped my eyes, wondering why I was so keenly watched by the strange woman. The man ceased his mutterings, and then a third bell was tapped. Every one picked up his knife and fork and began eating. I began crying instead, for by this time I was afraid to venture anything more.

But this eating by formula was not the hardest trial in that first day. Late in the morning, my friend Judéwin gave me a terrible warning. Judéwin knew a few words of English, and she had overheard the paleface woman talk about cutting our long, heavy hair. Our mothers had taught us that only unskilled warriors who were captured had their hair shingled by the enemy. Among our people, short hair was worn by mourners, and shingled hair by cowards!

We discussed our fate some moments, and when Judéwin said, "We have to submit, because they are strong," I rebelled.

20   "No, I will not submit! I will struggle first!" I answered.

I watched my chance, and when no one noticed I disappeared. I crept up the stairs as quietly as I could in my squeaking shoes, – my moccasins had been exchanged for shoes. Along the hall I passed, without knowing whither I was going. Turning aside to an open door, I found a large room with three white beds in it. The windows were covered with dark green curtains, which made the room very dim. Thankful that no one was there, I directed my steps toward the corner farthest from the door. On my hands and knees I crawled under the bed, and cuddled myself in the dark corner.

From my hiding place I peered out, shuddering with fear whenever I heard footsteps near by. Though in the hall loud voices were calling my name, and I knew that even Judéwin was searching for me, I did not open my mouth to answer. Then the steps were quickened and the voices became excited. The sounds came nearer and nearer. Women and girls entered the room. I held my breath, and watched them open closet doors and peep behind large trunks. Some one threw up the curtains, and the room was filled with sudden light. What caused them to stoop and look under the bed I do not know. I remember being dragged out, though I resisted by kicking and scratching wildly. In spite of myself, I was carried downstairs and tied fast in a chair.

I cried aloud, shaking my head all the while until I felt the cold blades of the scissors against my neck, and heard them gnaw off one of my thick braids. Then I lost my spirit. Since the day I was taken from my mother I had suffered extreme indignities. People had stared at me. I had been tossed about in the air like a wooden puppet. And now my long hair was shingled like a coward's! In my anguish I moaned for my mother, but no one came to comfort me. Not a soul reasoned quietly with me, as my own mother used to do; for now I was only one of many little animals driven by a herder.

III. The Snow Episode

A short time after our arrival we three Dakotas were playing in the snowdrift. We were all still deaf to the English language, excepting Judéwin, who always heard such puzzling things. One morning we learned through her ears that we were forbidden to fall lengthwise in the snow, as we had been doing, to see our own impressions. However, before many hours we had forgotten the order, and were having great sport in the snow, when a shrill voice called us. Looking up, we saw an imperative hand beckoning us into the house. We shook the snow off ourselves, and started toward the woman as slowly as we dared.

Judéwin said: "Now the paleface is angry with us. She is going to punish us for falling into the snow. If she looks straight into your eyes and talks loudly, you must wait until she stops. Then, after a

25

tiny pause, say, 'No.'" The rest of the way we practiced upon the little word "no."

As it happened, Thowin was summoned to judgment first. The door shut behind her with a click.

Judéwin and I stood silently listening at the keyhole. The paleface woman talked in very severe tones. Her words fell from her lips like crackling embers, and her inflection ran up like the small end of a switch. I understood her voice better than the things she was saying. I was certain we had made her very impatient with us. Judéwin heard enough of the words to realize all too late that she had taught us the wrong reply.

"Oh, poor Thowin!" she gasped, as she put both hands over her ears.

Just then I heard Thowin's tremulous answer, "No."

30 With an angry exclamation, the woman gave her a hard spanking. Then she stopped to say something. Judéwin said it was this: "Are you going to obey my word the next time?"

Thowin answered again with the only word at her command, "No."

This time the woman meant her blows to smart, for the poor frightened girl shrieked at the top of her voice. In the midst of the whipping, the blows ceased abruptly, and the woman asked another question: "Are you going to fall in the snow again?"

Thowin gave her bad password another trial. We heard her say feebly, "No! No!"

With this the woman hid away her half-worn slipper, and led the child out, stroking her black shorn head. Perhaps it occurred to her that brute force is not the solution for such a problem. She did nothing to Judéwin nor to me. She only returned to us our unhappy comrade, and left us alone in the room.

During the first two or three seasons misunderstandings as ridic-   35
ulous as this one of the snow episode frequently took place, bringing
unjustifiable frights and punishments into our little lives.

Within a year I was able to express myself somewhat in broken
English. As soon as I comprehended a part of what was said and done,
a mischievous spirit of revenge possessed me. One day I was called in
from my play for some misconduct. I had disregarded a rule which
seemed to me very needlessly binding. I was sent into the kitchen to
mash the turnips for dinner. It was noon, and steaming dishes were
hastily carried into the dining-room. I hated turnips, and their odor
which came from the brown jar was offensive to me. With fire in my
heart, I took the wooden tool that the paleface woman held out to
me. I stood upon a step, and, grasping the handle with both hands, I
bent in hot rage over the turnips. I worked my vengeance upon them.
All were so busily occupied that no one noticed me. I saw that the turnips were in a pulp, and that further beating could not improve them;
but the order was, "Mash these turnips," and mash them I would! I
renewed my energy; and as I sent the masher into the bottom of the
jar, I felt a satisfying sensation that the weight of my body had gone
into it.

Just here a paleface woman came up to my table. As she looked
into the jar she shoved my hands roughly aside. I stood fearless and
angry. She placed her red hands upon the rim of the jar. Then she gave
one lift and stride away from the table. But lo! the pulpy contents fell
through the crumbled bottom to the floor! She spared me no scolding
phrases that I had earned. I did not heed them. I felt triumphant in
my revenge, though deep within me I was a wee bit sorry to have
broken the jar.

As I sat eating my dinner, and saw that no turnips were served, I
whooped in my heart for having once asserted the rebellion within me.

IV. The Devil

Among the legends the old warriors used to tell me were many stories of evil spirits. But I was taught to fear them no more than those who stalked about in material guise. I never knew there was an insolent chieftain among the bad spirits, who dared to array his forces against the Great Spirit, until I heard this white man's legend from a paleface woman.

40   Out of a large book she showed me a picture of the white man's devil. I looked in horror upon the strong claws that grew out of his fur-covered fingers. His feet were like his hands. Trailing at his heels was a scaly tail tipped with a serpent's open jaws. His face was a patchwork: he had bearded cheeks, like some I had seen palefaces wear; his nose was an eagle's bill, and his sharp-pointed ears were pricked up like those of a sly fox. Above them a pair of cow's horns curved upward. I trembled with awe, and my heart throbbed in my throat, as I looked at the king of evil spirits. Then I heard the paleface woman say that this terrible creature roamed loose in the world, and that little girls who disobeyed school regulations were to be tortured by him.

That night I dreamt about this evil divinity. Once again I seemed to be in my mother's cottage. An Indian woman had come to visit my mother. On opposite sides of the kitchen stove, which stood in the centre of the small house, my mother and her guest were seated in straight-backed chairs. I played with a train of empty spools hitched together on a string. It was night, and the wick burned feebly. Suddenly I heard someone turn our door knob from without.

My mother and the woman hushed their talk, and both looked toward the door. It opened gradually. I waited behind the stove. The hinges squeaked as the door was slowly, very slowly pushed inward.

Then in rushed the devil! He was tall! He looked exactly like the picture I had seen of him in the white man's papers. He did not speak to my mother, because he did not know the Indian language, but his glittering yellow eyes were fastened upon me. He took long strides around the stove, passing behind the woman's chair. I threw down my spools, and ran to my mother. He did not fear her, but followed closely after me. Then I ran round and round the stove, crying aloud for help. But my mother and the woman seemed not to know my danger. They sat still, looking quietly upon the devil's chase after me. At last I grew dizzy. My head revolved as on a hidden pivot. My knees became numb, and doubled under my weight like a pair of knife blades without a spring. Beside my mother's chair I fell in a heap. Just as the devil stooped over me with outstretched claws my mother awoke from her quiet indifference, and lifted me on her lap. Whereupon the devil vanished, and I was awake.

On the following morning I took my revenge upon the devil. Stealing into the room where a wall of shelves was filled with books, I drew forth The Stories of the Bible. With a broken slate pencil I carried in my apron pocket, I began by scratching out his wicked eyes. A few moments later, when I was ready to leave the room, there was a ragged hole in the page where the picture of the devil had once been.

V. Iron Routine

A loud-clamoring bell awakened us at half-past six in the cold winter mornings. From happy dreams of Western rolling lands and unlassoed freedom we tumbled out upon chilly bare floors back again into a paleface day. We had short time to jump into our shoes and clothes, and wet our eyes with icy water, before a small hand bell was vigorously rung for roll call.

There were too many drowsy children and too numerous orders for the day to waste a moment in any apology to nature for giving her children such a shock in the early morning. We rushed downstairs, bounding over two high steps at a time, to land in the assembly room.

A paleface woman, with a yellow-covered roll book open on her arm and a gnawed pencil in her hand, appeared at the door. Her small, tired face was coldly lighted with a pair of large gray eyes.

She stood still in a halo of authority, while over the rim of her spectacles her eyes pried nervously about the room. Having glanced at her long list of names and called out the first one, she tossed up her chin and peered through the crystals of her spectacles to make sure of the answer "Here."

Relentlessly her pencil black-marked our daily records if we were not present to respond to our names, and no chum of ours had done it successfully for us. No matter if a dull headache or the painful cough of slow consumption had delayed the absentee, there was only time enough to mark the tardiness. It was next to impossible to leave the iron routine after the civilizing machine had once begun its day's buzzing; and as it was inbred in me to suffer in silence rather than to appeal to the ears of one whose open eyes could not see my pain, I have many times trudged in the day's harness heavy-footed, like a dumb sick brute.

50   Once I lost a dear classmate. I remember well how she used to mope along at my side, until one morning she could not raise her head from her pillow. At her deathbed I stood weeping, as the paleface woman sat near her moistening the dry lips. Among the folds of the bedclothes I saw the open pages of the white man's Bible. The dying Indian girl talked disconnectedly of Jesus the Christ and the paleface who was cooling her swollen hands and feet.

I grew bitter, and censured the woman for cruel neglect of our physical ills. I despised the pencils that moved automatically, and the one teaspoon which dealt out, from a large bottle, healing to a row of variously ailing Indian children. I blamed the hard-working, well-meaning, ignorant woman who was inculcating in our hearts her superstitious ideas. Though I was sullen in all my little troubles, as soon as I felt better I was ready again to smile upon the cruel woman. Within a week I was again actively testing the chains which tightly bound my individuality like a mummy for burial.

The melancholy of those black days has left so long a shadow that it darkens the path of years that have since gone by. These sad memories rise above those of smoothly grinding school days. Perhaps my Indian nature is the moaning wind which stirs them now for their present record. But, however tempestuous this is within me, it comes out as the low voice of a curiously colored seashell, which is only for those ears that are bent with compassion to hear it.

Acknowledgments

"Alien and Sedition Acts." This text follows that available from the Library of Congress (www.loc.gov). The text is in the public domain because it is a work of the US Government.

Jourdon Anderson, "A Letter to My Old Master." This text follows that available from the online collection of letters, Letters of Note (www.lettersofnote.com). The text is in the public domain because it was published before 1923.

Marcus Aurelius, "On Empathy." Adapted from George Long's 1862 translation of *Meditations*, previously published as *The Thoughts of the Emperor M. Aurelius Antoninus*. This text is in the public domain because both it and its translation were published before 1923.

Dewnya Bakri-Bazzi, "Sporting Faith," copyright © 2011 by Maria M. Ebrahimji and Zahra T. Suratwala. Reprinted with permission by White Cloud Press.

Lewis Buzbee, "Five and Dime." This text was first published in the Spring/Summer 2005 edition of *Black Warrior Review*, and subsequently in Lewis Buzbee's collection of short stories, *After the Gold Rush*, by Tupelo Press. Used by permission of Lewis Buzbee.

"Cherokee Memorial." This text follows that available from the History, Art, and Archives Collection of the US House of Representatives, history.house.gov. The text is in the public domain because it was published before 1923.

"Chinese Exclusion Act." This text follows that available from the Library of Congress (www.loc.gov). The text is in the public domain because it is a work of the US Government.

Wendy Chin-Tanner, "Empathy for the Devil: We Americans Should Stop Trying Not to Argue and Instead Try to Argue Well." This piece first appeared on *AlterNet* in 2017 (www.alternet.org). Used by permission of Wendy Chin-Tanner.

Kate Chopin, "The Story of an Hour." This text was first published as

"The Dream of an Hour" in *Vogue* on December 6, 1894. The text is in the public domain because it was published before 1923.

Christopher Columbus, excerpts from *Journal of the First Voyage to America*, 1492-1493. This text follows that available from *The Open Anthology of Early American Literature*, (openamlit.pressbooks.com). The text is in the public domain because it was published before 1923.

Kate Carroll de Gutes, "The Other Edition." This text was first published on May 4, 2017 (www.katecarrolldegutes.com). Used by permission of Kate Carroll de Gutes.

Rene Denfeld, "The Other Side of Loss." This text was first published on January 21, 2015 at *The Manifest-Station* (www.themanifeststation.net). Used by permission of Rene Denfeld.

Frederick Douglass, "What to the Slave Is the Fourth of July?" This text was first published in the 1855 edition of *My Bondage, My Freedom*. This text is in the public domain because it was published before 1923.

Ralph Waldo Emerson, "The Crime of Removal." This text follows that available from the *Cherokee Nation* (www.cherokee.org). This text is in the public domain because it was published before 1923.

George Estreich, "An Open Letter to Medical Students: Down Syndrome, Paradox, and Medicine". This text was first published in the April 2016 edition of the *American Medical Association Journal of Ethics*, vol. 18, no. 4, pp. 438–441. Copyright © 2016 American Medical Association. Used by permission of *AMA Journal of Ethics*.

Jenny Forrester, "Running Mountains." This text is excerpted from Jenny Forrester's 2017 memoir, *Narrow River, Wide Sky*. Used by permission of Jenny Forrester.

William Han, "I Spent the Last 15 Years Trying to Become an American. I Failed." This text was previously published at *Vox* on June 23, 2015 (www.vox.com). Used by permission of Vox Media, Inc.

A. R. Holcombe, "The Separate Street-Car Law in New Orleans." This text was first published in *The Outlook*, vol. 72, in 1902. The text is in the public domain because it was published before 1923.

Oliver Wendell Holmes, *Buck v. Bell*. This text that follows is available from the Library of Congress (www.loc.gov). The text is in the public

Library of Congress, www.loc.gov. The transcript of this speech is in the public domain because it is a work of an elected public official.

Ijeoma Oluo, "I Just Got Called Rasict, What Do I Do Now?" From *So You Want to Talk About Race* by Ijeoma Oluo, copyright © 2018. Reprinted by permission of Seal Press, an imprint of Hachette Book Group, Inc.

James Oppenheim, "Bread and Roses." This text was first published in *The American Magazine*, December, 1911. The text is in the public domain because it was published before 1923.

Demetra Perros, "Roots & Wings: A Memoir of Hope and Transformation." This text is excerpted from Demetra Perros's book and one-woman show, *Roots & Wings*. This is a copyrighted work and should not be reprinted without permission. This excerpt presents the research and ideas of its author. It is not intended to be a substitute for consultation with a health care professional. Used by permission of Demetra Perros.

Liz Prato, "The Terrible Things I Learned About My Dad: On Abuse and the People We Love." This text was first published on April 9, 2015 at *The Toast* (www.the-toast.net). Used by permission of Liz Prato.

Franklin Delano Roosevelt, "Statement on the National Industrial Recovery Act." This text follows that available from the Library of Congress, www.loc.gov. The transcript of this speech is in the public domain because it is a work of the US Government.

Margaret H. Sanger, "Impressions of the East Side." This text was first published in *New York Call*, September 3, 1911. The text is in the public domain because it was published before 1923.

Sonia Sotomayor, excerpt from "A Latina Judge's Voice." This text was first published as "Raising the Bar: Latino and Latina Presence in the Judiciary and the Struggle for Representation" in the *Berkeley La Raza Law Journal*. Copyright © 2002 by the Regents of the University of California. Used by permission of the Regents of the University of California.

"Standing Up for Our Law Enforcement Community." This text follows that available from the White House, www.whitehouse.gov. The text is in the public domain because it is a work of the US Government.

Sojourner Truth, "Ain't I a Woman?" This text was first published in
the 1887 edition of *History of Woman Suffrage*, Volume I, edited by
Elizabeth Cady Stanton, Susan B. Anthony, and Matilda Joslyn Gage.
The transcript of this speech is in the public domain because it was
published before 1923.

"Worried Man Blues." This text follows a traditional verse version of the
American folk song. It was first recorded in 1930 but is in the public
domain because the original was published before 1923.

Zitkala-Sa, "Impressions of an Indian Childhood." This text is excerpted
from Zitkala-Sa's 1921 collection *American Indian Stories*. The text is
in the public domain because it was published before 1923.

CPSIA information can be obtained
at www.ICGtesting.com
Printed in the USA
BVHW03s1131110818
524206BV00003B/66/P